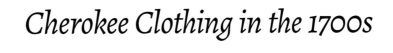

Cherokee Clothing in the 1700s

by BARBARA R. DUNCAN

MUSEUM OF THE
CHEROKEE
INDIAN

Cherokee Clothing in the 1700s

With Information from Previous and Following Centuries

MUSEUM OF THE CHEROKEE INDIAN PRESS • Cherokee, North Carolina

Publication of this work and the exhibit "Emissaries of Peace: The 1762
Cherokee & British Delegations," a We the People exhibit, have been
made possible by support from:
    The National Endowment for the Humanities
    The Cherokee Preservation Foundation
    First Citizens Bank
    Harrah's Foundation
    The Cannon Foundation

Further support for the Warriors of AniKituhwa, cultural revitalization
workshops at the Museum of the Cherokee Indian, and ongoing research by
Barbara R. Duncan were made possible by:
    The North Carolina Arts Council

Published by the Museum of the Cherokee Indian Press,
Cherokee, North Carolina
www.cherokeemuseum.org

Design & composition by BW&A Books, Inc., Durham, N.C.

Library of Congress Cataloging-in-Publication Data
Names: Duncan, Barbara R., author.
Title: Cherokee clothing in the 1700s : with information from previous and
    following centuries / by Barbara R. Duncan.
Description: Cherokee, North Carolina : Museum of the Cherokee Indian Press,
    [2016] | Includes bibliographical references and index.
Identifiers: LCCN 2016026691| ISBN 9780961059873 (hardcover : alk. paper) |
    ISBN 9780961059866 (softcover : alk. paper)
Subjects: LCSH: Cherokee Indians—Clothing. | Cherokee Indians—Social life
    and customs—18th century. | Costume design—North Carolina. | Indian
    craft—North Carolina.
Classification: LCC E99.C5 D838 2016 | DDC 975.004/97557—dc23
LC record available at https://lccn.loc.gov/2016026691

Cloth ISBN 978-0-9610598-7-3
Paper ISBN 978-0-9610598-6-6

20 19 18 17 16   5 4 3 2 1

Dedicated to the Warriors of AniKituhwa

Contents

List of Illustrations

11: Adornments

12: 1800s, 1900s, 2000s

Appendix E

Color Illustrations (follow page xvi)

Acknowledgments

First of all, my thanks go to the Warriors of AniKituhwa and to all the Cherokee people who inspired this research. Cherokee people asked me the questions that led me to search for this information, so that I could bring it back to the people. Marie Junaluska, Carmaleta Monteith, and Chrissy Arch helped set us on this path in 2002.

The original Warriors group included Walker Calhoun, John John Grant, Sonny Ledford, John "Bullet" Standingdeer, Bo Taylor, Daniel Tramper, Robert "Hoss" Tramper, and Will Tushka. Today they are joined by Mike Crowe Jr., Kody Grant, Micah Swimmer, Antonio Grant, and Ernest Grant and often accompanied by younger men including Jarrett Elk Wildcatt, Freddy Wilnoty, James "Last Bear" Wilnoty, Connor McCoy, and Wesley Welch. I am thankful to Walker Calhoun for his kindly guiding spirit and his sense of humor, and I honor his memory.

Bo Taylor, John John Grant, and John Standingdeer also participated in the research early on, and we made trips to the National Museum of the American Indian Cultural Research Center in Suitland, Maryland; to the University of Pennsylvania Museum of Anthropology and Archaeology in Philadelphia; and to the Library of Congress and National Archives and Records Administration in Washington, D.C. This research was invaluable to our present understanding of Cherokee clothing and other artifacts.

I give many thanks to the Pageant Committee of the Eastern Band of Cherokee Indians, who decided to adopt eighteenth-century dress for the Miss Cherokee, Teen Miss Cherokee, Junior Miss Cherokee, and Little Miss Cherokee pageants. As of this writing, committee members include Candi Martin, Lisa Wolfe Penick, Mollie Grant, Heather Younce, Ashleigh Brown Stevens, Yona Wade, Eleanora Thompson, Keredith Owens, and Samantha Crowe. Thank you to Kara Martin for wearing Mississippian-era clothing in the Miss Indian World pageant in Albuquerque and helping to start the revitalization of Cherokee weaving. Thanks to Nancy Maney and Johnnie Ruth Maney, who have sewed countless garments with thousands of stitches to bring this clothing into reality. Thanks to all the Cherokee women who wear this clothing so beautifully.

To the Colonial Williamsburg Foundation I am grateful for more than ten years of partnership and programs with the Museum of the Cherokee Indian, bringing the Warriors of AniKituhwa to Williamsburg in celebration of the original Cherokee delegations between 1741 and 1777. I thank the foundation for sharing artifacts with me and with members of the Eastern Band of Cherokee Indians. I appreciate Travis Henline, original director of the American Indian Initiative, who began this partnership in 2004. He encouraged our research on clothing by providing access to staff, information, and opportunities to participate in historical scenes beginning in 2005, when a few well-chosen gifts rounded out the wardrobe of the Warriors. My ongoing appreciation goes to Buck Woodard, current director of the Initiative, and to Timothy E. Sutphin, director of the Revolutionary City Programs, for continuing this partnership. Heartfelt thanks go to Brenda Rosseau, at the Costume Design Center, who volunteered her time, traveled to Cherokee in 2005, and instructed a group on the correct way of making an eighteenth-century shirt. I appreciate the boundless expertise and gracious answers of Mark Hutter, master tailor, as well. I also thank Frances Burroughs and Linda Randulfe, who created the "Emissaries of Peace" Electronic Field Trip and film; outfitting fifty Cherokee actors and extras in eighteenth-century clothing and accessories was quite a workout for me and the Museum, but the result was worth it.

Thanks to all the people who answered questions great and small over the years.

Wado, thank you, to Don Stroud and Margaret Raymond, citizens of the Cherokee Nation, who told me the truth about the Cherokee tear dress. They were there the night that it was created at the house of the Stroud family. I appreciate their honesty on this culturally sensitive issue.

Deborah Harding, collections manager at the Carnegie Museum of Natural History has been an important part of both researching and revitalizing the traditions of feather capes, finger weaving with beads, and textiles. I appreciate Deborah's research, her hands-on skills, and her ability to teach with humor and precision. She has made trips to Cherokee over the past ten years and has offered workshops through the Museum of the Cherokee Indian on finger weaving (oblique interlacing) with beads, making nets, creating feather capes, and twined-weft weaving. Her down to earth humor has endeared her to workshop participants, and her generous sharing of skills and expertise has made an impact on Cherokee traditions that will continue into the future.

I appreciate my colleagues who are dedicated to the search for truth about the eighteenth-century and whose delight in every detail is matched by their generous willingness to share. Thanks to Alan Gutchess at the Heinz History Center and R. Scott Stephenson at the Museum of the American Revolution. Their close examination of eighteenth-century American Indian artifacts around the world enabled them to tell me, when I really needed to know, how many stitches to the inch to use when sewing silk ribbon on wool trade cloth, and much more. Thanks also go to the Eastern Frontiers Conferences over the years. Thank you to Scott, Alan, and Michael Galban for confirming information on indigenous shirts.

Many thanks go to Penelope B. Drooker, first, for her outstanding archaeological research on fibers and textiles and, second, for a close reading of the introduction and chapters 1, 2, and 5 of this book. I appreciate her instruction on the finer points of archaeological terminology in this field. Deborah Harding also provided information on terminology for these chapters. All mistakes are mine.

For various and sundry inquiries, I thank Brett Riggs at the University of North Carolina at Chapel Hill Research Laboratories of Archaeology; Lynne Sullivan at the Frank McClung Museum, University of Tennessee, on Mississippian period clothing; Jefferson Chapman, director of the McClung; and Jonathan Leader, State Archaeologist, South Carolina.

On porcupines in the southern Appalachians, thanks for interesting discussions go to Thom Whyte at Appalachian State University; Bob Plott in Haywood County (if his dogs haven't found them, no one will); Anne Rogers at Western Carolina University; and the staff at the Oconaluftee Visitors Center, Great Smoky Mountains National Park.

Thank you, Steve Inskeep of National Public Radio, for illuminating the true footwear preferences of the Cherokee man known as Shoe Boots during the campaign at Horse Shoe Bend in 1814. Hessian boots are a long way from leggings, and thanks to your painstaking research for *Jacksonland*, I didn't make that mistake.

Thank you, my research buddies, Jerrid Miller, Cherokee Nation, for the journals of Louis Philippe; Carolyn Rice Nohria for the journals of Andre Michaux; and my sister Susan Ann Reimensnyder for librarian wizardry on obscure references.

Thank you to Ben DiBiase at the Florida Historical Society for a timely reply and a high resolution scan that enabled me to avoid perpetuating an error. A sketch previously identified as Mountain Cherokee turns out to have palm trees in the background, and the man is wearing Seminole garters. Thank you, Ben!

Thank you to the Cherokee Preservation Foundation, the North Carolina Arts Council, and the Eastern Band of Cherokee Indians for funding for this publication and the Warriors of AniKituhwa. The Cherokee Preservation Foundation funded the early efforts of the Warriors. The North Carolina Arts Council supports the Museum of the Cherokee Indian as a State Arts Resource organization, providing funding for some of my time on this project, for the Warriors, and for workshops. The Eastern Band of Cherokee Indians supports the Miss Cherokee pageants and the Warriors of AniKituhwa as cultural ambassadors.

The Museum of the Cherokee Indian is the home of this cultural revitalization of Cherokee clothing from the eighteenth century. "Emissaries of Peace: The 1762 Cherokee & British Delegations" is an exhibit that took on a life of its own and became a nexus of this research. This exhibit was funded by the National Endowment for the Humanities, the Cherokee Preservation Foundation, Harrah's Foundation, The Cannon Foundation, and First Citizens Bank.

At the Museum, my thanks go to past and present directors Ken Blankenship and Bo Taylor for seeing this project through. I thank Sharon Littlejohn for discussions on textiles and weaving. Thanks to Ethan Clapsaddle, Mike Little-john, and Nelda Reid in the Archives for tracking down some obscure articles, and sorting through microfilm, and scanning last minute requests. Thanks to Matt Tooni for working on the Documenting Endangered Languages project and transcribing some of Mooney's words from Manuscript 351, a difficult task. Thank you, Joyce Cooper, for comments on the manuscript as a whole.

Thanks to John Warner for outstanding photography of many of the artifacts pictured here. Thanks to Barbara Williams, Chris Crochetière, and all the staff at BW&A Books in Durham for their patience and their excellent work in making this a beautiful book.

Thank you to my daughter, Pearl, for being there through the whole process: being teased by the Warriors, trekking to many places, watching me sew, listening to me complain, dressing up a time or two, and even putting a linen diaper on your baby. You helped me more than you know.

To all the Cherokee people: *Nigohila ditsvyalihelitseho'i.* I appreciate you, always.

Barbara R. Duncan
Museum of the Cherokee Indian

Syacust Ukah, Cherokee Chief.
Painted by Sir Joshua Reynolds,
1762. Oils, 47 ½ inches x 35 inches.
Courtesy of the Gilcrease
Museum, Tulsa, Oklahoma.

Cunne Shote. Painted by Francis Parsons,
1762. Oils, 35 inches x 28 inches. Courtesy of
the Gilcrease Museum, Tulsa, Oklahoma.

Plate 1

Military Commission given to Oconostota by the French Governor of Louisiana, 1761. Note saved-list stroud breechclout. Courtesy of the U.S. National Archives and Records Administration.

Plate 2

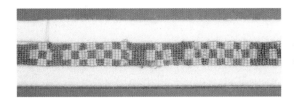

Rare Cherokee beaded garter given by Attakullakulla to Rev. Martin in 1758. Artifact about sixteen inches long total, with beads smaller than size 18. Courtesy of the Collection of Patrick R. Meguiar, now at East Tennessee Historical Society, Knoxville.

Bead necklaces, eighteenth century. Blue, white, and red glass trade beads. Courtesy of the Frank McClung Museum collection, University of Tennessee.

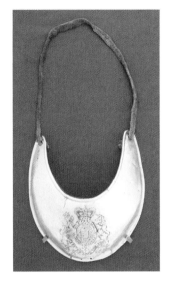

British military gorget. Eighteenth century. Courtesy of the National Museum of the American Indian collection.

Silver armband. French and Indian War period. Courtesy of the National Museum of the American Indian collection.

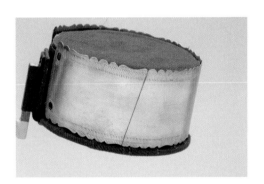

Silver Peace Medal of King George III. After 1760. Courtesy of the National Museum of the American Indian collection.

Daniel Cryn gorget. This gorget was made in New York in 1755 and found near the Nikwasi Mound in Franklin in 1887. Cryn may have participated in the Montgomery expedition against the Cherokees in 1760. Courtesy of the National Museum of the American Indian collection.

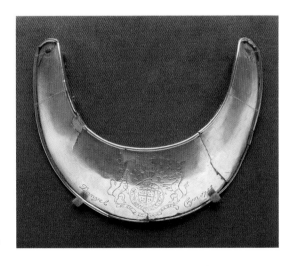

Plate 3

Portrait of George Lowry. Unknown Artist. Oil on canvas.
Courtesy of the Gilcrease Museum, Tulsa, Oklahoma.

Plate 4

"Happy While United" Indian peace medal. Made by Robert Scot, Richmond or Williamsburg, 1780, bronze, acc# 2009-6. Courtesy of the Colonial Williamsburg Foundation, Museum Purchase partially underwritten by the Lasser Family Fund of the Jewish Communal Fund.

Cherokee sash, ca. 1820 or earlier, navy and red trade cloth with white beads. 47½ inches long by 3½ inches wide. Full length. Courtesy of the Museum of the Cherokee Indian collection.

Cherokee sash, ca. 1820 or earlier, navy and red trade cloth with white beads. 47½ inches long by 3½ inches wide. Detail. Courtesy of the Museum of the Cherokee Indian collection.

Plate 5

Cherokee men's clothing, ca. 1750. Based on the list of gifts from General Geoffrey Amherst to the Cherokees in 1759. Silver gorget, linen shirt, wampum collar, match coat with bed lace, navy stroud leggings and breechclout with beadwork. Reproduction by Robert Scott Stephenson. Courtesy of the Museum of the Cherokee Indian collection.

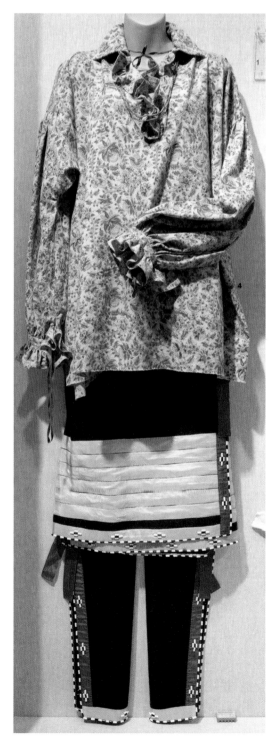

Cherokee women's clothing, ca. 1750. Based on descriptions ca. 1750. Shirt made of printed fabric from India, wrap skirt and leggings design based on eighteenth-century American Indian women's skirt in European collection. Reproduction by Robert Scott Stephenson. Courtesy of the Museum of the Cherokee Indian collection.

Plate 6

Ostenaco. Life-size figure from the exhibit "Emissaries of Peace: The 1762 Cherokee and British Delegations," created by Gerry Embleton and Robert Scott Stephenson. Ostenaco is wearing clothing described in 1762 during his audience with King George III. Courtesy of the Museum of the Cherokee Indian collection.

Museum of the Cherokee Indian permanent exhibit, life-sized figures portraying Ostenaco, Cunne Shotte and Woyi, 1762 based on the 1762 lithograph. Figures were made from life casts of Dale French, Dan McCoy, and John Standingdeer, Jr., left to right, created by Studio EIS, New York. Courtesy of the Museum of the Cherokee Indian.

Plate 7

Feather cape. White goose feathers simulate
swan feathers, individually fastened to a netting
of hemp yarn. Ties are made from hand-twined
dogbane. Created by Deborah Harding. Courtesy
of the Collection of Barbara R. Duncan.

Garter made by fingerweaving red and
blue wool with glass beads incorporated in the weaving (top). Garter
made by fingerweaving buffalo hair
with glass beads incorporated in the
weaving (bottom). The technique is
also called oblique interlacing. Created
by Karen George. Courtesy of the Collection of Oconaluftee Indian Village,
Cherokee Historical Association.

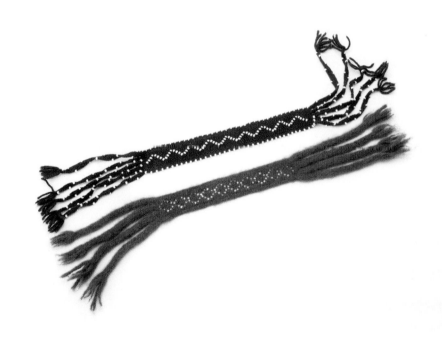

Plate 8

Warriors of AniKituhwa and friends on Palace Green at Colonial Williamsburg, 2005. Front row L to R: Daniel "Sonny" Ledford, David Owle, Daniel Tramper, Bo Taylor. Back row L to R: Travis Henline, Al Fugate, John Grant Jr., Robert "Hoss" Tramper, Walker Calhoun, John "Bullet" Standingdeer, Ty Oocumma. Photo by Barbara R. Duncan.

Plate 9

Warriors of AniKituwha and Miss Cherokees portray a Cherokee delegation of the mid-1700s in the Governor's Council Chambers at Colonial Williamsburg, 2010. Courtesy of the Colonial Williamsburg Foundation.

Plate 10

Marie Junaluska in feather cape and Walker Calhoun in chief's coat participating in "I Give You this Belt of Wampum," Colonial Williamsburg, 2006. Courtesy of the Colonial Williamsburg Foundation.

Plate 11

Amanda Wolfe, Miss Cherokee 2009. Feather cape of goose feathers dyed black on netted base made of hemp yarn. Linen shirt, trade silver earrings, bracelet, and brooches, red melton wool skirt and leggings with silk ribbon trim. River cane basket. Fingerwoven belt with beads. Knife sheath with beadwork, ribbon, and tin cones with dyed deer hair. Brain tanned moccasins with silk ribbon trim. Photo courtesy of the Eastern Band of Cherokee Indians.

Plate 12

Kody Grant in "So Far to Scioto," Colonial Williamsburg. Deer hair roach, red ochre paint, silver earrings, armband, and gorgets. Cotton printed shirt, wool vest, matchcoat trimmed with bed lace, and red wool leggings. Breechclout of saved-list stroud, buffalo hair garters with beads, deerskin moccasins. Courtesy of the Colonial Williamsburg Foundation.

Plate 13

Kara Martin, wearing circular feather cape with inset wild turkey breast feathers and reproduction of Clifty Creek skirt made by weft-twining hemp yarn. Reproductions by Deborah Harding. Photo by Jeremy Wilson Photography.

Plate 14

Warriors of AniKituwha and Miss Cherokees at the American Indian Heritage Celebration at the North Carolina Museum of History in Raleigh 2011. Front row L to R: Jade Ledford, Shakyra Bottchenbaugh, Deliah Esquivel, Dvdaya Swimmer, Kevonna Tushka, Kristina Hyatt, Abigail Taylor, Naomi Taylor. Middle row L to R: John "Bullet" Standingdeer, John Grant Jr., Will Tushka, Daniel Tramper, Alannah Tushka, Micah Swimmer, Stephanie Tushka, Nashoba Tushka, Ty Oocumma, Bo Taylor, Sonny Ledford. Far back row: Malaciah Taylor. Photo by Barbara R. Duncan.

Plate 15

Detail from engraved powder horn c. 1775. Cow horn. Length 12 ⅛ inches.
Elaborate and fully engraved powder horn depicts the plan of the Middle and
Lower Towns of the Cherokee nation; an Indian war dance; hunting scenes and
Fort Prince George. Note the Cherokee woman at left, wearing a knee length
skirt with triangular decoration, a short gown, and paint on her face.
Courtesy of the John and Marva Warnock Collection.

Plate 16

Introduction

The idea for this book came from Cherokee people. I have tried to be a collaborator in my work as a scholar, and this has led to projects that are much more interesting and fruitful than any I could have thought of. The Museum of the Cherokee Indian is my employer, and it represents the Eastern Band of Cherokee Indians; most of its board and staff are tribal members. As a tribal institution with the mission "to preserve and perpetuate the history, culture, and stories of the Cherokees," it, too, is responsible to Cherokee people.

In 2002 Marie Junaluska, a member of the Eastern Band, a Tribal Council representative, and a board member of the Museum, asked me, "Did we have a dance that we used to welcome people?" As a Tribal Council member, she had been welcomed with traditional dances by other tribes, including Maori and Hawaiian people performing the Haka. At the time, I was reading Henry Timberlake's memoirs in preparation for writing a grant proposal to fund an exhibit, and I remembered his description of the dance the Cherokees had welcomed him with in 1762 when he was an emissary of the British Empire. Between three and four hundred men, painted red and black, came to meet him as he approached Settico. They danced in "violent exercise" to drums, music, and yells from the crowd (2007, 19). Their leader, Cheulah (Tsula, the Fox), carried an eagle tail and a broadsword, which he flourished over Timberlake's head and stuck into the ground at the end of the dance. When Timberlake asked his interpreter about the intent of the dance, he was assured it was to bid him a "hearty welcome."

Junaluska, Chrissy Arch (Travel and Promotion), and Carmaleta Monteith, Ph.D., chose seven men and elder Walker Calhoun to recreate this dance, including James "Bo" Taylor who was an archivist at the Museum at that time. The process of bringing back the War Dance movements and music and the formation of the Warriors of AniKituhwa has been described elsewhere (Rogers and Duncan, eds., 83–116).

In December 2004, Colonial Williamsburg invited the Warriors of Ani-Kituhwa to dance on the Palace green. Cherokees had last danced there in 1777, and the event was electrifying. Their war whoops echoed off the brick walls of the Palace. Their songs in Cherokee language evoked the delegations of two and a quarter centuries earlier. Their movements were impressive. According to people in attendance, their humor and banter as they invited the crowd to

Warriors of AniKituhwa dance at Colonial Williamsburg, December 2004. Left to right: Sonny Ledford, Bo Taylor, Will Tushka, Bullet Standingdeer, Hoss Tramper. Photo by Barbara R. Duncan.

participate in some of the dances was unforgettable. They were painted red from head to toe, with individual black designs on some of their faces and bodies, and nearly all had long hair. They had made beautiful pucker toe moccasins of brain-tanned leather and were wearing only breechclouts and moccasins. Their silver armbands shone in the sun and their war clubs were authentic.

When the Warriors of AniKituhwa returned to Cherokee, the Tribal Council of the Eastern Band of Cherokee Indians, in February 2005 designated them official cultural ambassadors. The men present at Williamsburg and designated ambassadors included: Walker Calhoun, elder and singer for the group; John Grant Jr.; Daniel "Sonny" Ledford; John "Bullet" Standingdeer; James "Bo" Taylor; Daniel Tramper; Robert "Hoss" Tramper; and Will Tushka.

But a few of their clothing details didn't seem quite right. With the exception of the authentic breechclout of Black Watch tartan worn by Bullet Standingdeer, an allusion to the Cherokee victory in 1760 at Fort Loudoun, where some members of the Royal Highlanders were stationed, their breechclouts were patterned after those depicted on Mississippian gorgets. Their body paint included some Plains Indians motifs such as handprints and zigzags.

We began researching eighteenth-century clothing. I combed through all the primary sources and consulted with Robert Scott Stephenson, who is knowledgeable about the artifacts housed in European museums. Then I began sewing, by hand, breechclouts and leggings. Four of the Warriors of AniKituhwa and I attended the legendary Eastern Frontiers Conference, held in Akron, Ohio, on the material culture of Eastern Woodland Indians. Bo Taylor, Bullet Standingdeer, and I looked at artifacts related to dance and clothing in the National Museum of the American Indian in Washington, D.C., and the University of Pennsylvania Museum of Archaeology and Anthropology in Philadelphia. We talked with scholars, attended re-enactments, perused artworks, and benefitted from the expertise of Brenda Rosseau, Travis Henline, and others at Colonial Williamsburg.

By fall of 2005, the group was able to dress in historically accurate reproductions of eighteenth-century Cherokee clothing and participate in Colonial Williamsburg's historical interpretations, depicting one of the many Cherokee delegations to the colonial capitol. As the colonists had in the eighteenth century, Colonial Williamsburg gifted several shirts to the

Bo Taylor and John Standingdeer Jr. examine artifacts at the Smithsonian National Museum of History, 2005. Photo by Barbara R. Duncan.

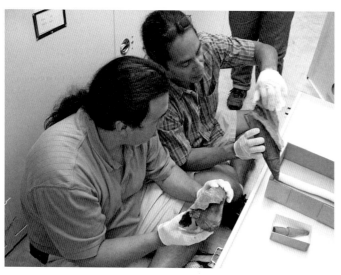

Warriors of AniKituhwa at the Capitol, Colonial Williamsburg, 2005. Photo by Barbara R. Duncan.

group. These gifts completed the men's clothing, which they wore when they performed dances and participated in historical dramas.

Since then, the Warriors of AniKituhwa have flourished. They have inspired Cherokees in Oklahoma and young people from many tribes. They have revitalized Cherokee dance traditions by bringing back dances that had not been seen in decades, by incorporating masks with their dancing, and by mentoring young Cherokee people. Their spirit, performance, and appearance represent the strength of the Cherokees. Their revitalization of the War Dance/Welcome Dance from the eighteenth century evokes a time when the Cherokees were a powerful tribe—larger than all the Iroquois nations combined in the North; ten times larger than their neighbors and war allies, the Catawbas; rivaled in their number of warriors only by the combined number of all the Muscogean people of the Southeast. This was a time when the Cherokees were players on a world stage, holding the balance of power in the French and Indian War for the Southeast; a time when their culture, traditions, and beliefs were still intact, still firmly rooted in the southern Appalachians. Their clothing helps to tell this story. In fact, their clothing is such an important part of this story that at every event they attend, they explain not only their dances but also their clothing and appearance.

Several years after the Warriors of AniKituhwa first performed at Colonial Williamsburg, the Miss Cherokee pageant committee adopted eighteenth-century Cherokee dress for women as part of the clothing for contestants. They observed historical standards but provided latitude so that young Cherokee women could make this clothing into their own, living tradition. Cherokee women compete annually, and those who are chosen often travel to dance with the Warriors of AniKituhwa, adorned with trade silver and feather capes. (See color photo, plate 15.)

Clothing and Culture

Clothing was an important part of daily life for the Cherokees in the eighteenth century; it reflected the changes taking place as the balance of population and land ownership shifted in the Southeast. It was part of the deerskin trade, which was of major economic importance to the colonies and to the American Indian tribes. Linda Baumgarten, a researcher of clothing, writes about clothing in general:

> Clothing provides a remarkable picture of the daily lives, beliefs, expectations, and hopes of those who lived in the past. People of all eras (including those living today), use clothing not only to meet functional needs, but also to communicate. The language of clothing speaks of status, occupation, aesthetics, social cohesiveness, propriety, and a host of other meanings, subtle and overt. (Baumgarten, viii)

Articles of clothing, cloth, silver armbands, and gorgets were given to the Cherokees at meetings to discuss trade and military alliances, and these gifts symbolized the relationship between Cherokees and the colonies of South Carolina and Virginia. Colonial governors and military officers understood the importance of cementing relationships with the Cherokees through gift giving. When Cherokee men came to fight as allies, they were given guns, powder, lead shot, and tomahawks, but they were also given clothing for themselves and for Cherokee women. For example, in 1759, General Jeffrey Amherst offered the following to Cherokees and Catawbas to go to war for at least three months:

> At first fitting them out to War. Guns: One to each Man that wants it, or to him that does not, either 6 yards of Callicoe for a Jacket and Petticoat or 8 yards of ¾ Garlix for two shifts for his Wife. . . . At their return from War . . . To reward for particular Services . . . Supposing 10 to be killed or taken, or Service equivalent, & to give in Consideration of each, 2000 Wampum, one silver Gorget, one Arm Band, & 2 Wrist Bands. (Mays 2009, 74–77)

Although these items were, in one sense, payment for military service, they also represented a relationship. This is illustrated by an incident in 1753, when the "Emperor of the Cherokees" was assaulted and badly beaten by Virginians on his way home from Williamsburg. He was so offended that he burned all the clothes and presents that Governor Dinwiddie had just given him, thus demonstrating the end of their relationship.

Looking at clothing gives us a picture of the daily lives of Cherokee people in the 1700s. It reveals their choices in a time of political, social, and environmental change. Cherokee people were using new materials to make clothing in their traditional patterns, such as the men's leggings, women's wrap skirts, and mantles. When they traded for cloth, they were making choices about what was beautiful, appealing, and economically justified. They used this new cloth

(far left) A silver gorget based on a traditional Cherokee design was inscribed "South Carolina" to reinforce the alliance, about 1756. Courtesy of the Frank McClung Museum collection.

A silver bracelet inscribed SC for "South Carolina" dates to about 1756. Approximately 1 ¼ inches wide. Courtesy of the Tommy Beutell collection.

in their own ways and to suit their own needs. For example, they used red and blue woolen stroud cloth to dye other fabrics, and they unraveled the threads to use in weaving belts and garters. Cherokee people adopted items of clothing that suited their needs and tastes, such as the English men's linen shirt, but they used these items in ways that seemed useful to them. For example, women wore these linen shirts as well. In addition, they used them as patterns for making shirts for themselves of printed cloth. They decorated these shirts with breast buckles (round silver brooches, also known as ring brooches) in their own style. Cherokee clothing of the eighteenth century is distinctly different from that of the nineteenth century, when European/American clothing was more fully adopted.

Looking at clothing also conveys the remarkable contrast between Cherokee culture and European culture of the colonial and federal periods. In European culture, clothes clearly represented the social and economic status of the wearer, much as they do today. On the other hand, Cherokee clothing speaks not of status but of the unimportance of status in Cherokee culture. In this way and others, Cherokees had a more democratic society than even the young America. James Adair, who lived with the Chickasaws and Cherokees from about 1735 to about 1770, stated:

> *Martial virtue, not riches, is their invariable standard for preferment; for they neither esteem, nor despise any of their people one jot more or less, on account of riches or dress. They compare both these, to paint on a warrior's face; because it incites others to a spirit of martial benevolence for their country, and pleases his own fancy, and the eyes of spectators, for a little time, but is sweated off, while he is performing his war-dances; or is defaced, by the change of weather.* (69)

For the Cherokees, "riches or dress" were no more important than paint on a warrior's face, which quickly wore off. William DeBrahm, architect of Fort Loudoun, who lived in the Cherokee Overhill Towns in 1756, further confirms this, saying, "The Indians have no Distinction of Dress among themselves" (109).

For the Cherokees, clothes, rather than status, represented identity and relationships. When they adopted a person from outside the tribe, they took his or her old clothes away and gave him or her new clothing representing their identity as a Cherokee person belonging to a family and clan. In the ceremony to cement "perpetual friendship," two people danced while taking off and exchanging every item of clothing. Then, when dressed in the other's clothes, they both pledged "To regard and treat him as himself while he lived" (Payne V4:101).

Tattoos indicated the deeds of warriors. Cherokees achieved status through actions, not through clothing. James Adair says of southeastern American Indians, "They are all equal—the only precedence any gain is by superior virtue, oratory, or prowess; and they esteem themselves bound to live or die in defense of their country" (Adair, 375).

Among the Cherokees, only three positions were represented by distinctive clothing: the peace chief, the spiritual leader, and the war chief. These offices had distinctive colors and items associated with them: a crown of white feathers for the peace leader; yellow feathers for the *uku* or spiritual leader; and red for the war leader, as described by Payne and Butrick about 1830. In addition, the Beloved Women and Beloved Men of the Cherokees each carried a white swan wing that represented his or her position.

The Indian Fashion: Southeastern or Cherokee?

This work focuses on Cherokee clothing in the 1700s. A certain style was common to all the tribes of eastern America during this period: moccasins, breechclouts, leggings, wrap skirts for women, shirts for men and women, shaved heads for men, and long hair for women. This was known during the time as "the Indian fashion." Certain natural materials were commonly available, depending on the environment of the tribe: hides, feathers, native cloth, twine, and quills. The trade materials available in the eighteenth century also were commonly available to many tribes: linen shirts, woolen cloth, silver breast buckles, and ball and cone earrings. But within these possibilities, tribes developed their own preferences for colors, materials, and trade items; these preferences have been documented as early as the seventeenth century.

It is possible, however, to determine what Cherokees were wearing during the 1700s. The descriptions of Henry Timberlake are invaluable because he visited the Cherokees only. Likewise, William Bartram's visit to the Cherokee Middle Towns provides descriptions of clothing specific to the Cherokees. Descriptions by James Adair, Andre Michaux, and others mention the Cherokees by name. Lists of gifts to the Cherokees from the military provide valuable information, particularly because the military chose gifts based on the known preferences of different tribes. The Colonial Records of South Carolina likewise contain lists of presents given to Cherokees during their official visits to Charleston. They provide fascinating accounts of negotiations and haggling between Cherokee and colonial officials to set prices of goods; they also provide lists of goods stocked by traders who traveled to the Cherokees. Portraits of Cherokees on visits to London in 1730 and especially in 1762 provide additional information. Archaeology from eighteenth-century Cherokee towns fills out the picture. It is possible to know what Cherokees were wearing, what colors they preferred, what items came from their environment, what items they were trading for, and what items were given to them. In addition, eighteenth-century artifacts from archaeological digs provide very specific details about their location, if not their cultural affiliation. In regard to archaeological artifacts, I define as Cherokee those artifacts that came from the original Cherokee territory: the southern Appalachians.

Sometimes the primary sources of this period do not distinguish among the southeastern tribes. Often, for example, Adair and Bartram describe southeastern Indians in general. Most museums do not specify the tribe from which artifacts from this period originated. I have tried to be very specific about which sources in this text refer to the Cherokees. I feel this is necessary for accuracy.

I also hope that, by indicating which descriptions apply generally to the southeastern people, this work may be of use to other tribes of the Southeast who are interested in their clothing of the eighteenth century. Specific artworks, ethnographic descriptions, and archaeological artifacts can be found for each of the southeastern tribes, and these provide information on clothing specific to that tribe.

The *Monthly Chronicler*, 1762, describing the meeting between Ostenaco, Cunne Shotte, Woyi, and King George III. Courtesy of the Museum of the Cherokee Indian collection.

Contents and Scope

This book also presents Cherokee clothing of the 1700s within a larger historical context. The first chapter looks at what we know about the clothing of the earliest people in the southern Appalachian mountains, more than thirteen thousand years ago, up to the 1700s. The second chapter describes the general appearance of Cherokees during the 1700s. The following chapters on eighteenth-century clothing are organized by parts of the wardrobe: breechclouts, leggings, skirts, shirts, matchcoats, feather capes, moccasins, belts, sashes and garters, and adornments. Each short chapter includes a description of what Cherokees were wearing, sources of information about these items, and references. Some practical information is included as well, at the end of each chapter, for those who want to re-create this clothing. The final chapter looks briefly at Cherokee clothing in the 1800s, 1900s, and 2000s. The transitional period about 1800 and the clothing of the Removal Era are described, along with late-nineteenth-century clothing of the Eastern Band of Cherokee Indians. Twentieth-century clothing is briefly described, including the ribbon shirt and the tear dress, items that symbolized Cherokee identity from about 1970 into the twentieth century but were never part of traditional dress. Finally the chapter looks at the role of clothing in the process of cultural revitalization.

End material includes glossaries, appendices with additional material, a bibliography, and an index. There is a glossary of Cherokee words pertaining to eighteenth-century clothing and a glossary of clothing terms in English. Other appendices include a list of goods and prices in 1751, a list of goods and prices in 1762, a list of trader John Vann's inventory and his license, and a chart of plant and animal fibers used by the Cherokees in textile weaving.

This book does not cover many topics related to eighteenth-century material culture. Such descriptions can be found in the same sources used to procure information about clothing. Pipes and their ornamentation; feather wands used in dancing; feather painting by specialists; weapons; and ceremonial wampum belts are not within the scope of this work. Personal items made of wampum are mentioned in the chapter on jewelry and adornments.

I use the terms "clothing," "dress," "garments," and "wardrobe" to describe what Cherokees were wearing. The term "costume" has pejorative meanings for some Cherokee people, so I avoid that term. The term "regalia" usually refers to clothing and items made for powwow dancing.

Methodology

My methodology for assembling this information involved finding information from all possible sources and academic disciplines and cross-referencing it. Using this multidisciplinary approach is like being a detective. More than one person told me that I would never find enough information to determine what Cherokees were wearing in the eighteenth century.

The sources are there, however, if you are persistent. My sources included information from archaeological reports, artifacts in museums and private collections, written accounts from the 1700s, artwork from the 1700s, oral traditions, records from the colonial governments in South Carolina and Virginia, letters on microfilm in the Archives of the Museum of the Cherokee Indian, military records from the 1700s, and newspapers and journals from America and Great Britain. If two independent sources confirmed a piece of information, then I considered it valid, as long as there was no cultural evidence to the contrary.

One such example began with the list of gifts from General Amherst to the Cherokees in 1759 (Mays 2009). Among the presents to Cherokees who had greatly distinguished themselves in battle was twenty-four yards of bed lace (a kind of sturdy decorative tape). From other research I had already confirmed that the typical matchcoat was about two yards long or a little less. This meant that a match coat decorated with this amount of bed lace would have eleven or twelve stripes. One of the engravings of Cherokees in London shows Ostenaco, who held the highest war rank, *Sgiagvsta*, with eleven stripes on his match coat. This suggested to me that visual and written sources could be used to confirm each other.

My efforts were aided by the research that went into creating the exhibit "Emissaries of Peace: The 1762 Cherokee & British Delegations," and by the knowledgeable scholars who served as a panel of experts for the Museum. I especially appreciate the knowledge and generous spirit of Robert Scott Stephenson, Ph.D., who shared information from his experience with artifacts scattered throughout Europe and from twenty years of researching the material culture of the Eastern Woodland Indians. I thank the many others who contributed to this effort in the Acknowledgments. All mistakes are my own.

The ideal source would be a time capsule containing the complete ensembles of a Cherokee man's clothing and a Cherokee woman's clothing from 1762. This does not exist. To use material generated by different academic disciplines, I employed the method I developed about the year 2000 while teaching at the Cherokee History and Culture Institute at the Museum of the Cherokee Indian. Every discipline has something to contribute as well as its limitations. In this

Ostenaco. Courtesy of the Amon Carter Museum collection.

method I take into account the possible contributions and limitations of each discipline, and look at what can be determined by comparing data across disciplines. In thinking critically about this information, I aimed to remain centered within a Cherokee point of view.

Let's look at woven garters and sashes in the 1700s as an example.

- Archaeology: Archaeologists tell us that in burials dating to the eighteenth century in the Cherokee area, many beads are found in the area around the knee. They cannot tell us how these beads were fastened together: oblique interlacing with wool or other yarn; warp twining; weft twining; interlacing with two sets of elements (threads); or simply strung on a cord. They cannot tell us why people wore these beads, what they thought about them, what name they had for them, or what language they used to speak that name.
- Artifacts: Artifacts in museums, although extremely rare, provide several examples of sashes identified as Cherokee that are beaded sashes woven (or twined) with two perpendicular sets of elements (warp and weft). Other sashes identified as southeastern are made with beads incorporated in oblique interlacing, known as fingerweaving among Cherokee people. These artifacts can tell us more about techniques of weaving, upon close examination, but cannot tell us anything about how frequently these sashes were used or worn. Many of these artifacts are in Europe and are difficult to access.
- Historical sources: An ethnographic account from James Adair (2005) states that southeastern Indian women wove buffalo hair with beads and wore these sashes around their legs. Bartram and others describe Cherokee and other southeastern women weaving sashes and garters for men to wear. Artwork from the period shows Cherokee men wearing garters that

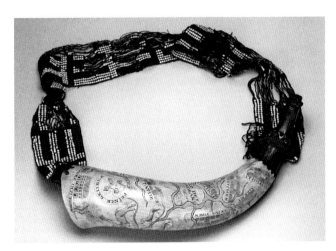

Cherokee powder horn with sash made of glass beads and wool yarn, made either by weaving or by twining the wefts around the individual beads. Courtesy of the John and Marva Warnock collection.

Southeastern sash, National Museum of Natural History. Photo by Deborah Harding. Courtesy of the Smithsonian National Museum of Natural History collection.

Souvenir of Tokouo, 1819. Felix Marie Ferdinand Storelli, after a sketch by Antoine-Phillipe d'Orleans, Duc de Montpensier, 1797. Oil on canvas. Courtesy of the Ridley Wills II collection.

appear to be fingerwoven with beads incorporated or that feature woven or twined beadwork similar to wampum bands. These men also wear decorated bands around their necks that may be beadwork, though not enough detail is provided to tell. Portraits of Cherokees in the 1830s show elaborate beaded belts and sashes.

· Oral traditions: Cherokee traditions carried fingerweaving (oblique interlacing) with beads incorporated (not sewn onto the surface) into the twentieth century when the last practitioner, Mary Shell, passed away in the 1990s.

What can we conclude from this?

1. Cherokee men wore sashes, belts, and garters. Evidence comes from archaeology, artifacts, artwork, and ethnographic accounts.
2. Cherokee women wore garters around their legs. Evidence comes from archaeology and ethnographic accounts.
3. Cherokee fabric production techniques included beads woven on yarn with an underlying warp-and-weft technique. Evidence comes from powder-horn straps in museum collections identified as Cherokee.
4. Cherokee weaving techniques included fingerweaving (oblique interlacing) with incorporated beads. Evidence comes from ethnographic accounts and the ongoing oral tradition that existed through the twentieth century.

To draw further conclusions, we have to jump to using evidence from other tribes. For example, to understand how the beads were woven into straps and sashes with yarn in warp and weft interlacing (two elements woven together) we have to look at techniques practiced by the Sauk and Fox or wampum band construction as practiced by the Northern Iroquois tribes (Orchard, 1929, 95–97).

We also have to remember there are gaps in all the records. Although no known artworks depict Cherokee women in the 1700s, one painting from 1819 does portray Cherokee women at Toqua, and this painting was based on a sketch from 1797, by Louis Phillippe, Duc Du Montpensier, which has been lost. Their clothing matches many of the written descriptions of Cherokee women's clothing in the 1700s, including one woman who wears a baby tied to her back and a garter below one knee. Paintings from the 1700s of women from other tribes match some of the general styles described for them and for Cherokee women, with some tribal differences.

In this book I try to clearly state what I know to be true, what I am extrapolating from other tribes to fill in gaps in the record, and what is speculation. A further source of information comes from trying to re-create some of these items and discovering the properties and limitations of particular materials.

Context of Clothing

When interpreting data in this way, it is important to know as much as possible about the history and culture of one's subject, in this case, the Cherokees in the eighteenth century. We all are biased, consciously and unconsciously, by our own culture and by our historical period. Knowing as much as possible about the eighteenth-century world and the viewpoint of the Cherokees then and now can help overcome some of this bias. This is what I mean when I say I strive to stay centered within the Cherokee point of view. For example, women of the twenty-first century might take exception to the fact that Cherokee women made elaborate belts and sashes for men but did not wear the belts themselves. To a modern feminist, this might seem to be evidence of inequality, and she might insist that it's just that we don't have data about the women wearing belts—it's just a gap in the record. She might insist on wearing her own finger-woven belt, and in doing so, she is continuing this tradition in her own way; all traditions continue because they have meaning for the present generation. But for the traditional Cherokees of the eighteenth century, men's and women's roles were different and both were respected. Both were seen as essential to the survival of the people. Wearing different clothing items did not mean that men had more respect or a higher status; they were just different. For the Cherokees, everyone was equal; all status was based on deeds and accomplishments. Understanding this makes it easier to see and accept the data.

Historians talk about the "middle ground" or "common ground" in the backcountry of the eighteenth century. (The word frontier" was not commonly used until after 1800.) This is a fairly recent approach by ethnohistorians, and it basically shows that American Indians influenced Europeans, as well as being influenced by them. Cherokees were valued by George Washington because they could teach his troops how to fight the tribes who were allies of the French. Cherokee crops and agricultural techniques were important to settlers for food.

Many sought knowledge of medicinal plants from the Cherokee—and not only about ginseng for trade to China but also how to use native plants for healing.

In this dynamic exchange, I contend that European goods did not leave the Cherokees and other tribes in awe. From the beginning of their trade with Europeans, the tribes were very selective about what items they would trade for. The most important item was guns, followed by lead, powder, and flints. The deerskin trade, in my opinion, could be characterized as an arms race, to use modern phraseology. During the 1650s a tribe from the Lake Erie area, the Westos, acquired guns before any other tribes and swept through the east, taking slaves from many tribes and selling them to the English to work on sugar plantations in the West Indies (Meyers 2009, 81). Under that threat, all tribes wanted guns. The arrival of similarly armed Europeans and the spread of guns to other tribes only intensified the need for guns. The Cherokees' expertise in hand-to-hand combat and their strength and skill with bow and arrow could not protect them from a bullet fired from a distance.

Cherokees were not newcomers to trading. Extensive trade networks date back more than eight thousand years, to the early Archaic period, when Cherokees traded items to and from the Great Lakes, the Gulf coast, and the Atlantic coast. They maintained extensive trade networks through the 1500s and beyond.

According to historian Robert Scott Stephenson,

The 18th-century 'Indian Fashion' incorporated items that could only be obtained through exchange and gift-giving. Selectively adopting these manufactured goods, native peoples developed a rich style of dress, but one that still drew on traditional practices, ideas, and technology. (2006, 10)

Some historians have stated that the Cherokees became dependent on trade. They were certainly dependent on European sources for guns and ammunition. Colonel James Grant stated, after his battle with Oconostota and several thousand Cherokees in 1761, that the Cherokees would have won had they not run out of ammunition after being unable to trade with the British for a year.

I disagree, however, with depictions of the Cherokees as dependent on European goods. One of the primary sources of information on the dependence of Indian tribes on trade is the account of John Lawson, a surveyor in the Carolinas. He traveled mainly in the piedmont, where European influence arrived much earlier. He did not visit the Cherokees.

Evidence shows that the Cherokees adopted materials and trade items selectively and fit them into their traditional ways of farming, making clothing, and living. For example, they continued to raise their traditional crops, with their traditional methods of interplanting and working the fields but substituted iron hoes for those of shell or bone because they lasted longer. They continued to prefer stews and soups to fried food but added iron pots, which they used alongside their clay pots.

This substitution of new materials in traditional forms shows up clearly in clothing traditions. Men's shirts made of leather or native cloth were replaced by those made of linen. Women's skirts were made in the same knee-length, wrap-around style, but of wool or linen rather than native cloth or leather.

I believe there were reasons for all the choices the Cherokees made. Some of those reasons may have been personal preference. They may have *liked* the new materials the way we like new clothing items and changing fashions. Other factors may include the population loss they suffered in that century. Between 1690 and 1790, four smallpox epidemics ravaged the Cherokee nation, which lost between 30 and 50 percent of its people each time. Population loss was so severe that Ostenaco mentioned it in his speech to King George III: "Our women are bearing children as fast as they can." People with specialized knowledge about weaving cloth and producing other items may have had to focus on basic survival.

Women may have felt that it took less time to raise corn, or to have their brothers or husbands kill deer to trade for cloth than it took to process mulberry bark and other fibers, to spin, and to weave. Creating cloth from natural fibers is a time-consuming process. Penelope Ballard Drooker, an anthropologist, estimates that a woman who devoted four hours a day for three hundred days to gathering, processing, spinning, and weaving could produce "one coarse and one relatively fine garment for herself every year, plus three mantles or blankets for other members of her family, plus two large storage bags, all undecorated" (1992, 168).

The Cherokee skirt described in chapters 1 and 5 was forty-six inches wide by twenty-four inches long and estimated to have required 144 hours of labor to create. A length of stroud for a matchcoat was approximately seventy-two inches by forty-eight inches. This larger piece of cloth cost between two and three buckskins. Cherokee women may have judged that buying this cloth was far cheaper in time and effort, even when women were processing the deerskins for trade. Both men and women may have felt that deer were a renewable resource, having always been available to the towns in nearby herds, some of which may have been semi-domesticated. Or perhaps Cherokee women, as expert cloth-makers, appreciated the quality of English stroud, with its vibrant red and blue colors, warmth, and weight, or appreciated well-made linen for its body and durability.

The survival of many traditions from the eighteenth century to the present day—river cane basket making, pottery making, bow and arrow making, blowgun and dart making, traditions of food preparation, gardening, gathering, and more—testifies to the fact that Cherokees were not totally dependent on trade goods. Many of these traditions were part of daily life well into the twentieth century. Some of these traditions survive today because their products are sold to tourists and to art collectors.

Clothing and Diplomacy

In addition to the importance of clothing items in the deerskin trade, the exchange of clothing was an important part of diplomacy. Before every meeting on trade or military alliances, presents of clothing were given to the Cherokees (and to other tribes). When Cherokee men went to fight as allies of the British, they were given specific presents before they fought, which often included guns if they did not have them. Another set of presents was given when they returned from fighting; special items such as silver armbands and gorgets were given to the men who had distinguished themselves by killing or taking prisoner large numbers of the enemy.

Lists of these items give us detailed information about exactly what was available to the Cherokees. For example, the list of gifts from General Amherst to the Cherokees in 1759 specifies blue stroud for leggings and matchcoats, and green and yellow silk ribbon (Mays). This list also includes the Catawbas, who often went to war along with the Cherokees on the same campaigns during the French and Indian War, although the Cherokees far outnumbered the Catawbas by this time, perhaps by as many as ten to one.

At meetings to set prices for the Indian trade between South Carolina and the Cherokees in November 1751, for example, gifts included:

> For the Raven a scarlet Coat, waistcoat and Breeches, ruffled shirt, gold-laced hat, Shoes, Buckles, Buttons, Stockins and Gartring, Saddle, one of the best Guns, Cutlass, a Blanket and Knife, a Peice of Stroud, 5 yards of Callico, ten Yards of Embossed Serge. . . . For the Good Warrior of Estatoe, the same as the Raven's Son, with one of the best Guns and a Saddle and Cutlass, but no Commission, with 5 yards of Callico, a silk Handkerchief, and a Trunk for his wife. (McDowell 1958, 161)

By this time, colonial governors and military leaders had learned that they needed to please the Cherokee women also. Gifts for Cherokee women were regularly part of these exchanges, and at the same meeting, the following items were specified: "For each of the women now in Town 5 yards of embossed Serge, some Beads, needles, thread, Ear Bobs, Cadiz, Gartering, Ribbons, Sicsors, Pea Buttons, Ivory Combs, and Trunks" (McDowell 1970, 162). In addition, at this particular meeting, sixty-four guns and sixty-four hatchets were to be distributed by the "Head Men." A significant portion of the gifts was sent directly to the Cherokee Nation: "400 Weight Powder, 800 Bullets, 2,000 Flints, 10 Pounds Vermilion, one Gross Brass Nailes" (162). Readers interested in more details can find the prices set at this meeting transcribed in appendix C and prices set in 1762 in appendix D.

Note on Cherokee Language Terms

Throughout the text, I try to provide Cherokee language terms for clothing and other items associated with clothing. Some of these terms come from the word list generated by William Gerard DeBrahm, who visited the Cherokee Overhill Towns in 1756 as the surveyor for Fort Loudoun. Other sources include lists dating between 1819 and 1900. Some words are still in use and can be found in modern Cherokee dictionaries.

Cherokee words are represented in English phonetics, using the syllables from the printed syllabary chart of 1828. Consonants are pronounced as in English. Vowels are pronounced as follows:

a = ah as in father

e = a as in late

i = ee as in see

o = oh as in spoke

u = u as in rule

v = uh pronounced nasally as in "Uh huh"

Note on Eighteenth-Century Sources

English spelling and capitalization were not consistent in the eighteenth century. I have retained the spelling from original sources as they were published, in an effort to provide some of the flavor of the times.

The names of fabrics, trims, and garments may be modern, but they often refer to different items. For example, "callico," "calico," or "calicoe" does not refer to the printed, densely flowered cloth we know today but to a lightweight cotton cloth that originated in Calcutta, India. This cloth could be plain, printed, or dyed. Printed fabric was either chintz (as we know it today) or sprigs of flowers presented on a light background. Lace does not refer to the kind of transparent, delicate lace we think of today but to a sturdy tape or trim that was usually at least an inch wide, woven in solid or multi-colors with a raised pattern. Laces also referred to the metallic trims used in military uniforms, so that a "laced hat" refers to a tricorn hat decorated with metallic trim, usually gold, about an inch wide or less. For more information on fabric and clothing terms in English language, see the glossary at the end of the book (appendix A).

1 *Paleolithic through Mississippian: Not All Buckskin!*

Cherokee elders say that they have lived in these mountains forever. They say that the Creator put them here and gave them their language and traditions. They say that their ancestors live in the streams and inside the mountains and that if you're quiet for a long time you can hear them singing.

In the 1880s, John Ax and Swimmer, whose Cherokee name was Ayuini, told the beginning of the Cherokee creation story like this:

> The earth is a great island floating in a sea of water, and suspended at each of the four cardinal points by a cord hanging down from the sky vault, which is of solid rock. When the world grows old and worn out, the people will die and the cords will break and let the earth sink down into the ocean, and all will be water again. The Indians are afraid of this. (Mooney 1900, 239)

Back beyond anyone's memory, cords held the world in place. Making cords, or cordage, is one of the oldest ways people worked with fibers. Thread, yarn, cords, and rope differ only in their thickness and the number of elements twisted together. They can be created using the same technique of twisting two strands (or more) of fiber together. This technique was used with sinew, hair from animals, and long plant fibers. In the oldest way of doing this, you hold two strands with your left hand and pull gently while using your right hand to move the two strands outward across your thigh, imparting twist to them. The two strands are then rolled together in the opposite direction to create a stronger, more functional product. These cords or threads (depending on their size) can then be used to construct woven, twined, linked, looped, interlaced, and knotted fabrics.

"Stone Age toolmakers grasped the significance of twisting, which increases strength by diverting part of any tensile load into lateral pressure," according to a textile historian (Schoeser 2003, 10). This is another example of Cherokee technology.

cords

twining

nets

bags

slippers

cloth

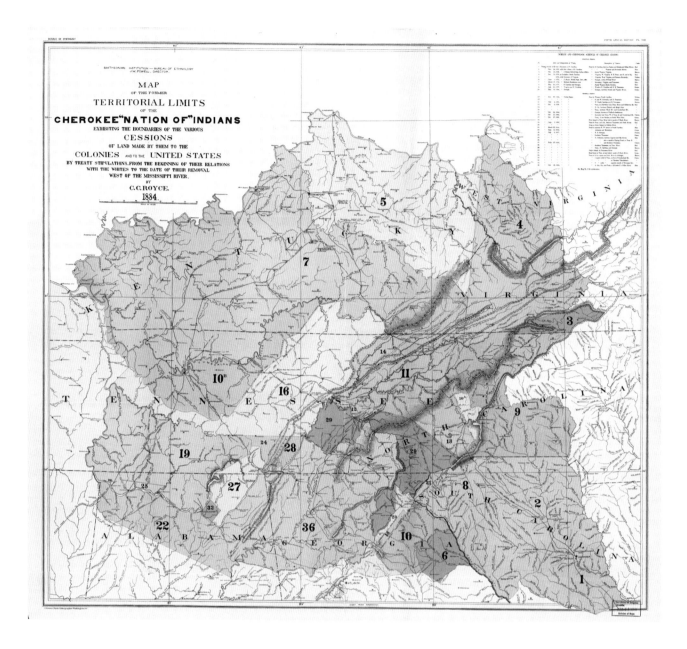

Map showing original Cherokee homeland in parts of eight present-day states. Smithsonian *Bureau of American Ethnology Fifth Annual Report* Plate VIII. Map by Charles C. Royce, 1884.

This chapter looks at artifacts and evidence from the geographical area historically associated with the Cherokees, as delineated by Cherokee treaties drafted between 1721 and 1883 and compiled by Charles Royce between 1884 and 1887. This approach to defining the cultural affiliation of artifacts is in keeping with the traditional view of Cherokee elders, with the permanent exhibit at the Museum of the Cherokee Indian, and with recent revisions (2010) to the Code of Federal Regulations in regard to public lands and tribal affiliation.

Archaeologists do not usually attribute tribal affiliation to ancient people, referring to them instead, in southeastern North America as "Paleo Indians," "Archaic Indians," "Woodland Indians," or "Mississippian Indians." These can be misleading designations, however, since the terms "Paleo," "Archaic," "Woodland," and "Mississippian" do not refer to people who shared one language and culture and thought of themselves as a related group. These terms refer to time periods during which certain practices, technologies, and social organization were typical over large regions. During these time periods, people in the Southeast lived in groups and were speaking distinct languages that evolved into the languages known today as Cherokee, Creek, Choctaw, Chickasaw, and others.

Paleolithic Period, 12,500–about 8000 BC

People have lived in the southern Appalachians for more than fourteen thousand years, according to archaeologists. Scholars continue to push back these dates as new evidence comes to light that contradicts the theory that ancestors of all American Indians came across the Bering Strait 12,500 years ago. Recent work by archaeologists from the University of South Carolina shows people living at the Topper site (about one hundred miles from Cherokee, North Carolina, within the original Cherokee area) more than sixteen thousand years ago and perhaps as long as fifty thousand years ago. Scholars refer to the time when people used primarily stone tools as the Paleo period. During this period, people lived by hunting animals, including now-extinct megafauna, and gathering plants as they moved across the land from season to season. The most characteristic artifacts surviving from this time are large, beautifully made projectile points, but other types of items were made and used as well. Cultures around the world used remarkably similar stone tools and technology during this time.

Stone spear points and tools survive in the earth for a long time, but organic materials do not. We know that people in the southern Appalachians made beautiful spear points from local stone because these are found throughout the mountains. We know that these people hunted mastodons because a mastodon vertebrae was found that was worked by stone tools. We know they worked animal hides, possibly tanning them, because some stones are shaped into scrapers, with one sharp edge for scraping and a blunt edge for holding the tool safely in the hand. You can see these early tools on display at the Museum of the Cherokee Indian.

We can say that plants likely constituted a large part of the diet of early people in the southern Appalachians. Jefferson Chapman writes of the people who lived in what is now east Tennessee: "Paleo Indians have been often referred to as big game hunters, focusing on the now-extinct large animals of the last Ice Age. A more accurate description would be to call them generalized foragers who supplemented their diet of plant foods and small game with an occasional opportunistic killing of a mastodon" (Chapman 2009, 5).

It is possible that their knowledge of plants extended to making cordage. We can only infer, however, that these ancestors of the Cherokees had cords because they had to have a way to attach spear points to shafts; they could have used plain sinew. Since they had needles, we can infer that they were sewing with some kind of thread, but again, this could have been sinew. Since they had tools for scraping hides, we assume that they were wearing leather clothing, shaped and held together in some fashion.

We have very little evidence of how the people in the southern Appalachians used plants during this period. We do not know whether they made plants and other fibers into clothing, because no materials have survived. Impressions of cords and cloth on clay hearths are the only clue to actual creation of mats and bags; they come from a slightly later time but show skilled cord-making, twining, and netting that could have predated the clay hearths of 7500 BC.

If we look at other cultures from this same period, however, we see that the indigenous people of South America were making cords and weaving threads into cloth more than eleven thousand years ago. Recently carbon dating was used to determine the age of textiles found in a cave in the Andes mountains in Peru. Tests were performed on the cords and twined fabric. In addition, the cave contained bundles and coils of materials that had been processed and were ready to be woven. These artifacts date to between 12,100 and 11,080 years ago (10,100–9080 BC). Fragments of three "finely woven" textiles were found along with fifty-three lengths of cord (Jolie et al.).

At the same time, people in Europe were twisting plant fibers into cords, based on artifacts found in the Lascaux caves in southern France. Further evidence comes from the depiction of skirts made of twined cords hanging from a belt worn by women, in small, carved stone figures. The earliest artifacts of this kind in Europe are twenty thousand to twenty-seven thousand years old.

These techniques were used in southwestern America, about twelve thousand years ago, and in South America, more than eleven thousand years ago. They could have been of the same age in the southern Appalachians, but no archaeological evidence remains.

Archaic Period, 8000–1000 BC

As the climate warmed after the Ice Age ended, plants, animals, and the culture of the people changed. At this time people in the southern Appalachians used plant fibers to make rope, cords, and threads, which they then used to create nets, bags, cloth, shoes, blankets, and mats. They were experts in techniques of knotting, twining, and interlacing, which they employed in many inventive ways. Archaeological evidence is scarce because fibers are perishable, but we can see that nets were commonly used for fishing, because of the large number of net sinkers carved of stone found in archaeological sites.

The ancestors of the Cherokees were making very fine cord and using it to make fabric as early as 7500 BC—more than 9,500 years ago, not long after the time of the textiles found in Peru. In contrast to numerous artifacts made of stone, no textiles remain from this period. We do, however, have evidence of textiles impressed on clay that was hardened by fire. People regularly camped at and returned to a site on the Little Tennessee River west of the Great Smoky Mountains called Icehouse Bottom, near present-day Vonore, Tennessee. Here we find evidence of the some of the oldest textiles in eastern North America, dating to more than nine thousand years ago. They are so finely made that archaeologists have concluded that people had been making cords and thread from plant fibers for far longer.

About 9,500 years ago people at Icehouse Bottom pressed patterns from these twined fabrics and knotted nets onto the damp clay they were using to form

Knot used to create nets for fishing and bags. This is the type of knot preserved on ancient hearths at Icehouse Bottom in the original Cherokee territory. Courtesy of *American Antiquity.*

their hearths. Hearths were about three feet across, shaped like a pancake about one and a half inches thick, and made of local red clay. At Icehouse Bottom, twenty-nine hearths bore impressions of twined fabric and netting. Charcoal on these hearths enabled archaeologists to date them. The impressions were transferred from woven mats and large round bags made of plant fibers. Clay hearths from other sites dating from the Archaic period were also impressed with textiles, including the Cold Canyon site on Alarka Creek, near present-day Cherokee, North Carolina (Riggs 2015).

Two types of fabrics were impressed in the clay. The fabric-making techniques that were used could also have been used to make clothing, baskets, mats, bags, cradles, and fishnets (Chapman and Adovasio 1977, 622). Although the plant fibers could not be identified, a large number of plant species native to the site could have been used to make the twined materials.

The first type of fabric was knotted netting, probably from a net or bag. This technique employed a sheet bend knot (also called a weaver's knot) to create a row of knotted loops, onto which a second row of knotted loops was added, and so on. The result was an open diamond mesh. The plant fiber had been twisted into a single-ply (one-strand) thread about one millimeter in diameter. This is less than one-thirty-second of an inch. The thread was twisted clockwise.

The second type of fabric present was likely from large mats or large round bags. This fabric was made by twining; two wefts were twisted around one warp at a time. Warps are the vertical threads and wefts are the horizontal threads. Both were two-ply, meaning two strands were twisted together to make the thread. In this case, the average diameter of the warp was 1.25 millimeters, and the average diameter of the weft was 2.25 millimeters, a little more than one-sixteenth of an inch. The average gap between the rows of twining wefts was 7.73 millimeters, about three-eighths of an inch.

Twined weft-weaving technique. This technique is preserved on ancient hearths at Icehouse Botton in the original Cherokee territory. Courtesy of *American Antiquity.*

Close up of knot used in weaving. Reproduction by Deborah Harding. Courtesy of the Museum of the Cherokee Indian collection.

Round bag made with netting technique. Reproduction by Deborah Harding. Courtesy of the Museum of the Cherokee Indian collection.

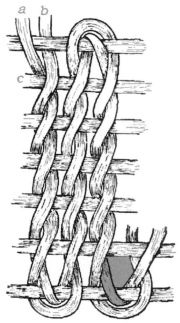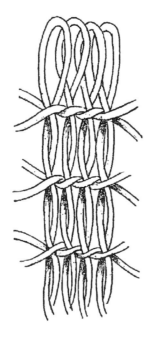

Schematic of twining from Orchard.

Shoes made of twined and interlaced fabric, twined bags, twined cloth from clothing or blankets, and fabric-production materials dating to between three and four thousand years ago have been found in caves in and near the southern Appalachians. They were made from fibers from the cattail plant (*Typha* spp.), from the inner bark of the pawpaw (*Asimina triloba*) and basswood (*Tilia americana*) trees, from Indian hemp (*Apocynum cannabinum*) or dogbane (*Apocynum androsaemifolium*), and from a species of native grass. The constant environmental conditions, and, in some cases, the mineral salts of the caves preserved these fiber artifacts. Salts Cave, Kentucky, in Mammoth Caves National Park, about one hundred miles north of Nashville and within the original Cherokee territory, is one such site.

One of the fabric fragments discovered in such a cave was originally about a quarter inch thick and could have been used as clothing or a blanket. It was made by simple twining, with the weft rows very close together and completely hiding the warp. The thread was made from six or eight strands of plant fibers twisted together, a much heavier thread than was found in the bags and slippers.

One of the bags was approximately 9½ inches wide and 7¾ inches high. It was made using an open weft-twining technique, with the rows of weft twining about half an inch apart. Both warp and weft were twisted. Edges were finished with a six-strand braid. Both the braid and weft were dyed. A smaller bag, about two inches wide and two-and-a-half inches deep, without braided edges was made using the same technique (Orchard 1920).

Similar techniques were used to make the footwear found in these caves. Techniques varied with the materials used. Cattail fibers, which are large and coarse, were worked in a plain checker weave (1/1 interlacing) to make a basic sandal.

Finer fibers, such as those from Indian hemp (*Apocynum spp.*), were used to make several styles of slip-on shoes, which were "a graceful, comfortable form which could hardly be improved in modern shoe-making" (Orchard 1920, 14–15). These shoes were made using a weft-twining technique where the weft twining rows completely cover the warp threads. The threads were made of slightly twisted material, and the warp and weft were of the same material. A single warp thread was used, and pairs of weft threads were twisted around it, a technique called "plain twining."

The surfaces of the slippers showed two different patterns. In one, the twining twists all appeared to slant in one direction. In the other, the slant direction alternated in each row, producing a chev-

Bag made by twined-weft technique, from plant fibers, more than 2,000 years old, from a cave in the original Cherokee territory. From William Orchard. Courtesy of the National Museum of the American Indian collection.

ron design. More slippers were found with this design, which may have been preferred because it is easier to produce on a small object. A chevron pattern occurs automatically when the person doing the twining turns the fabric 180 degrees whenever she starts a new row, in order to always twine in the same direction, but continues to twist the weft pairs in the same direction. This is easier and faster than twining first left-to-right then right-to-left, or changing the twist direction with every row.

In one type of slipper, first a rectangular piece of fabric was twined to approximately fit the foot. The edges of the fabric were turned up at the heel and fastened to create the sides of the shoe. This resulted in a point projecting slightly at the base of the heel. At the front of the foot, the fabric was brought together and the warp ends braided together to create a seam that extended from the toes to the instep. The top warp strands on each side of the shoe were apparently pulled tight to fit the foot, and a finishing edge was added that extended over the instep and might have been used to tie the shoe tightly onto the foot. Another style followed the same basic pattern, although the fabric over the front of the foot bulged outward, possibly to improve the shoe's fit, create a different style, or provide insulation for the foot, if, for example, the bulges were stuffed with plant fiber (Orchard 1920, 15).

Sandals and slip-on shoes found in other parts of the country have even earlier dates. Slip-on shoes and sandals made from twined plant fibers date back more than 8,000 years. They have been found in a cave on the Missouri River in present-day central Missouri, in caves in the Ozarks, on the Colorado Plateau, and in Oregon (Kuttruff et al. 1998).

Shoes made by twining, braiding, and lacing, from plant fibers, from a cave in the original Cherokee territory. From William Orchard. Courtesy of the National Museum of the American Indian collection.

Woodland Period, 1000 BC–900 AD

About three thousand years ago Cherokee people began living year round in towns along rivers throughout the southern Appalachians. They made pottery, cultivated gardens, fished, hunted with bow and arrow, traded, and smoked stone pipes carved in the shapes of birds, animals, and people. According to linguistic scholars they were already speaking Cherokee in a form that was distinctly different from other Iroquoian languages.

They were accomplished at cloth production, as we can see from the fabric impressed upon pottery. People wore gorgets carved out of stone and the upper part of conch shells. They wore necklaces of shells from the Atlantic and Gulf coasts. We can assume they continued to use knotting and twining techniques to make bags, cords, fishnets, shoes, and other functional items.

The earliest Cherokee pottery, which was made about three thousand years ago, was commonly impressed with fabric or stamped with wooden paddles that had cords wrapped around them. This created a textured surface that conducted heat more efficiently and also made the surface easier to grip. This is another example of Cherokee technology. On the Swannanoa River, at the Swannanoa site east of present-day Asheville, North Carolina, this pottery was first excavated and studied, and so the archaeologists who first studied it gave it the name of this site. The same style was common throughout the Cherokee area,

Swannanoa pot, fabric impressed. From Warren Wilson site, Swannanoa, North Carolina. Note the resemblance to a mud dauber's nest, as in the Cherokee legend of the origin of pottery. Courtesy of the Research Labs of Archaeology University of North Carolina at Chapel Hill collection.

This fragment of cloth from the Spiro Mound, from the Mississippian period, shows oblique interlacing, known today as fingerweaving. Courtesy of the National Museum of the American Indian collection.

with fabric-stamped pottery of the same age found in northeastern Tennessee at Phipps Bend, northeast Georgia (referred to as Kellog ceramics), and east Tennessee (referred to as Watts Bar ceramics). Iroquois potters in the north were making pottery stamped with paddles wrapped with cords (referred to as Vinette ceramics) at about the same time.

During this period in Central America, Mayan people were using fibers from cotton and maguey to create very finely woven fabrics that were also dyed. Recent archaeological discoveries revealed hand-woven cloth with more than eighty weft yarns per inch.

Mississippian Period, 900–1600 AD

About 900 AD Cherokee people began living in towns with central mounds, extensive cornfields, gardens, and orchards. They continued to make cords, cloth, and other materials by twisting, twining, knotting, and interlacing. They made skirts, mantles, blankets, and bags using these techniques. They were trading items within a network that reached from the Atlantic coast to the Gulf coast and far to the north, although the copper used during this period came from the Southeast.

Fabric-making techniques included warp twining, weft twining, and finger-weaving (oblique interlacing). By using different sizes of threads for warps and wefts, by choosing different plant fibers, and by adjusting the spaces between threads, Cherokee women made cloth of varying thicknesses, textures, and patterns that was suited to its purpose. They used dyes from plants to create patterns of color. Twined fabrics with different structures and patterns of texture were created by using the following techniques: (1) Plain open twining; (2) Plain twining with grouped weft rows; (3) Plain twining with transposed interlinked warps; and (4) Plain twining with transposed crossed diverted warps. In the larger Mississippian region, women were making twined garments with a variety of patterns, many of which survive as impressions in pottery (Drooker 1992). At one site, people made designs in twining and also created complex openwork fabrics that to a modern observer look like European bobbin lace. About eighty miles west of Nashville, Tennessee, on the edge of the historic Cherokee territory, at the Stone site, impressions were found of a particularly complex fabric, similar in appearance to European lace (Drooker 1991, 1991b). These designs survive because they were impressed on pottery.

In addition, people at this site made openwork garments with complex openwork patterns created by twining and braiding. Similar complex, lace-like fabrics have been found in burials at Etowah Mounds (west-central Georgia) and Spiro Mounds (Oklahoma) (Drooker 1991; 1992, 200–203).

Beautiful artwork from this period survives in the form of drawings engraved on shell gorgets, carved stone figures, effigy pipes, and a few pottery figures. Some depict clothing. Some organic clothing items survive as artifacts uncovered by archaeology. Written descriptions from Europeans at the time of contact with Cherokees (1540) and other tribes (1492–1550) provide additional information.

Cherokee men wore breechclouts and sometimes an additional garment cov-

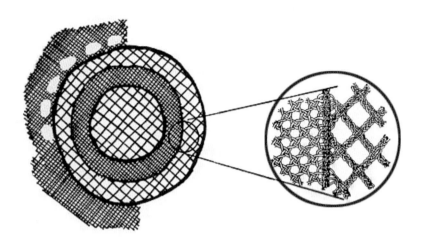

ering the lower body, on top of the breechclout. They wore leggings, moccasins, hip-length shirts, mantles, and feather capes. Some leather and cloth mantles were painted with designs. Some feather capes were made of long wing feathers, as depicted on shell gorgets. They wore garters of shell or woven fabric, sometimes incorporating shell beads, around their ankles and just below the knee. They wore armbands around their upper arms and wrists. They wore copper plates or feathers in their hair. In their ears, they wore spools carved from stone, about one inch in diameter, with wood in the middle, covered with mica, copper, or shell, or they wore long earpins of bone. Necklaces were made from columnella shell from the inside of conchs, from olivella shells, marginella shells, bone, and small worked shell beads, and from (more rarely) freshwater pearls. They made pendants, wristbands, and neck plates of copper. Carved shell gorgets depicted snakes, birds, and other animals from myths and legends, such as the water spider bringing fire and the *uktena,* the giant monster snake that could kill with its gaze. They wore their hair long, tied up in a bun, with a forelock hanging down in front, sometimes adorned with beads. They carried pouches shaped like an inverted teardrop as well as functional rectangular bags. They wore tattoos and body paint.

Cherokee women wore short, knee-length skirts. They wore a mantle over one or both shoulders made of leather, cloth, or feathers. The cloth and leather mantles were sometimes painted. They wore leggings and moccasins in cold weather. They wore bracelets on their wrists made from copper or shells, and garters below the knee, sometimes with shell beads. They wore necklaces of freshwater pearls, shell beads, columnella shells, marginella shells, bones, and carved shell gorgets. Their ears were pierced for ear spools or ear pins. When DeSoto's expedition was traveling through what is now north Georgia, they described the women who gave them food—corn cakes and green onions—as wearing white skirts and mantles made of mulberry cloth. Perhaps these were Cherokee women bearing gifts of bean bread and ramps.

Textile artifacts from this period are very rare, but two Cherokee skirts survive. Mineral salts in the earth preserved these, under a small rock overhang on Clifty Creek in Morgan County, Tennessee, about forty-five miles west of present-day Knoxville. Two skirts, a bag, skeins of thread, and other items were wrapped in a river cane mat, and all were well preserved. These have not been dated, but they are typical of clothing from the Mississippian period, as well as earlier, clothing. They provide a detailed look at Cherokee fabric and basketry production.

One skirt is a rectangle with a drawstring, a style that continued through the eighteenth century, when new materials were used in the same pattern. The warp (vertical) threads are twenty-four inches long. This would have been the length of the skirt from waist to knee. The weft (horizontal) rows are forty-six inches long, and this would have been the length that wrapped around the woman's hips, with or without some overlap. Along the starting edge, the warp threads are looped to create a tunnel for a drawstring. This would have been worn at the waist. On the opposite edge, the warps extend from the fabric and form short decorative loops. On the sides, (selvages) the weft threads extend in concentric loops, presumably for decoration. The skirt was originally described as "coarse, pliable, yellowish-gray stuff, woven in the twined style so common all over America":

> *The fiber was doubtless derived from the native hemp, and the strands are neatly twisted. . . . The [woof strands] have been passed through with the length of the cloth in pairs, which are twisted half around at each intersection, inclosing the web strands in alternating pairs. . . . These twined strands are placed but three-eighths of an inch apart, the web being so close that the fabric is but slightly open. (Holmes 1884, 31)*

Early European writers assumed that native textiles were made of hemp (*Cannabinum spp.*) because this material was so common in Europe and was used for the same purposes—making ropes, nets, and cloth. The hemp plant, commonly known as the *Cannabis* species, was native to Europe, however, and did not exist in North America until colonists imported it. Colonists called any plant used for making cords and cloth "hemp," regardless of its actual identity.

Photo of Clifty Creek skirt by Shan Goshorn.

Photo of Kara Martin in Clifty Creek Skirt and feather cape. Reproductions by Deborah Harding. Photo by Scott McKie Brings Plenty / Cherokee One Feather. Courtesy of the Museum of the Cherokee Indian collection.

The plants, often called "Indian hemp," that were used by the Cherokees and other tribes were from the species *Apocynum*. One of its varieties is *Apocynum cannabinum*, but it is not the same as the *Cannabis* species, which includes *Cannabis sativa,* known for its psychoactive properties. Their appearance and their properties are distinctly different. "Indian hemp," as used by the Cherokees, is *Apocynum cannabinum*, which does not have psychoactive properties. Its close relative, dogbane, *Apocynum androsaemifolium*, was also used. Its medicinal properties are anti-inflammatory, like aspirin.

Research in the twentieth century showed that this particular skirt was most likely made from fibers harvested and spun from the stem of the woods nettle,

Girl's skirt from Holmes.

Laportea canadensis (Whitford 1941). The Cherokees used several species of nettle, including the woods nettle, the slender nettle (*Urtica gracilis*), and the stingless nettle (*Boehmeria cylindrica*), which made especially fine thread.

The Cherokees used at least sixteen different plants and three kinds of animal hair to make fibers (Whitford). In addition to those mentioned above, they used the inner bark of the mulberry (*Morus rubra*), which was prepared by soaking, beating, soaking again in lye, and bleaching in the sun before spinning. All plants were treated in some way before being spun. Milkweed fibers were used, including those from the butterfly weed (*Asclepias tuberosa*). In the eighteenth century, milkweed species were commonly known as silkweed. Threads made from this plant were used to make Iroquois wampum belts. Other plants definitely used by the Cherokees include: basswood, cattail, jute, palmetto, pawpaw, richweed, and yucca. Animal fibers definitely used by the Cherokees included those from buffalo, possum, and bear. Fibers from rabbit hair were also used in the Southeast. More plant and animal fibers may yet be identified by future research on the rare textiles surviving in museum collections. For a table of plant and animal fibers documented as used by the Cherokees, see appendix F.

Until they were about ten to twelve years of age, Cherokee children wore very little clothing except for a mantle or blanket. Then, boys began wearing the breechclout and girls the knee-length skirt. The second skirt recovered from the Clifty Creek site may have belonged to a girl. It has a woven band with strings hanging down in what looks like a long fringe. It may have been created that way, or its wefts may have been dyed and then deteriorated before the undyed warps. Some dyes, like walnut, are acidic and tend to speed up deterioration. If the wefts were dyed and the warps undyed, then openly spaced twining rows would have created bands of color. The garment's length from waist to knee is twenty inches. Its measurement around the waist, a narrow band with drawstring, is thirty-four inches.

European Contact, 1500–1650

As the Hernando de Soto expedition approached Cofitachequi, on the edge of the historic Cherokee territory, his chroniclers recorded:

Indian men and women came forth . . . to receive them, and the women were clothed in white and made a fine appearance. . . . The white clothes with which the women were clothed were mantles, apparently of homespun linen, and some of them were very thin. They make the thread of them from the bark of the mulberry tree, not the outside, but the intermediate layers; and they know how to make use of it and to spin it, and to dress it as well and to weave it. They make very fine mantles, and they wear one from the girdle [waist] down, and another fastened on one side with the end over the shoulders . . . and the thread is of such a quality that one who was there assured

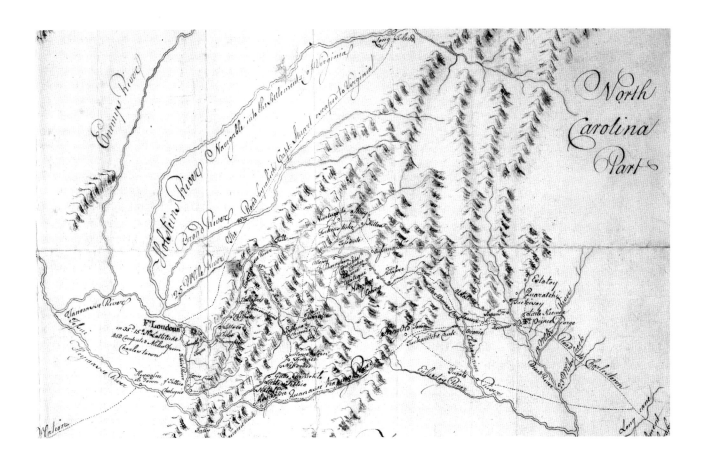

me that he saw the women spin it from that mulberry bark and make it as good as the best thread from Portugal, that women can get in Spain for their work, and finer and somewhat like it and stronger. (Swanton 1946, 451)

Detail from map by Captain John Stuart, 1764, showing Cherokee towns. Courtesy of the British Library.

Between 1500 and 1650, European diseases killed perhaps ninety percent of the American Indian people in North and South America (Dobyns 1983). This resulted in the disappearance of whole nations of people and in the end of the Mississippian way of life in the Southeast. Some tribes merged to survive. Others abandoned the edges of their territory and gathered their remaining population in towns near the center of their original territory. Cherokees lived in towns along the rivers of the southern Appalachians.

By the beginning of the eighteenth century, these towns were concentrated in four areas:

- Overhill Towns: West of the Appalachians, in present-day east Tennessee, the Overhill towns were clustered along the Tennessee and Hiwassee Rivers.
- Valley Towns: East of the Appalachians, the Valley towns were concentrated between present-day Murphy and Andrews, North Carolina, along the Hiwassee and Valley Rivers, and included "out" towns along the Cheoah River and Santetlah Creek, in present-day Snowbird.
- Middle Towns: About fifty miles further east, the Middle Towns stretched fifty miles from the headwaters of the Little Tennessee River in

present-day Rabun County, Georgia, to its turbulent intersection with the Nantahala Mountains, creating a stretch of gardens, fields, and orchards so dense that William Bartram could hardly find a path for his horse without stepping on cultivated ground; outlying towns on the Tuckaseegee River included the mother town of Kituhwa.

- Lower Towns: Further east and south, in present-day South Carolina, Cherokee towns were numerous on the headwaters of the Savannah, Tugaloo, and Keowee Rivers; outlying towns in present-day Georgia included Nacoochee.

Although each town had its own independent government, in the eighteenth century Cherokees realized that dealing with Europeans required a more centralized approach. Towns kept their independence but began thinking of themselves in these geographical terms. Each town had one set of leaders for peace (the "white" government) and one for war (the "red" government), guided always by a spiritual leader, the *uku*, and by the beloved men and beloved women. Other towns extended throughout north Georgia, Tennessee, and even into Virginia.

The Cherokee population at the beginning of the eighteenth century is estimated to have been more than forty thousand people in sixty towns. In 1693 Cherokee leaders traveled to Charleston to complain that slavers were capturing Cherokees and selling them in Charleston. This visit was followed by a smallpox epidemic that killed between 30 and 50 percent of the Cherokee population. Thus began a century that included four smallpox epidemics causing an overall population loss of tens of thousands of people, and the loss of perhaps seventy-five percent of the original land base through wars and treaties. At the end of the eighteenth century, by about 1800, Cherokee people did remain, speaking Cherokee language and practicing their traditional religion, dances, and ways of life. But greater changes were yet to come.

The changes of the 1700s are reflected in Cherokee culture, including in the clothing of the people. During this time, Cherokee people continued to trade, as they had for millennia. They continued to make clothing from the materials in their environment, as they had for millennia. They continued to make choices that reflected their cultural traditions and individual preferences. In doing so, they created styles of clothing that reflected this changing time while remaining uniquely Cherokee.

2 *Cherokee Appearance in the 1700s*

The "Indian dress" or "Indian fashion," as it was called in the eighteenth century, was based on centuries-old traditions among the Cherokees and other tribes. In the early 1700s, Cherokees wore clothing based on traditions of the 1600s and earlier. They began substituting new goods obtained in trade, using them to make their familiar styles. For example, men wore breechclouts made of stroud cloth instead of leather. Women made their knee-length wrap skirts of wool stroud instead of weft-twined cloth made from mulberry bark or nettles. They used European items in Cherokee ways, applying decorations of silk ribbon and bedlace to matchcoats and wrap skirts. They began adding new items to their wardrobes, such as the linen shirt. They wore these items in ways distinctly different from Europeans; we could say they "Cherokeeized" them. On occasion they dressed in outfits of primarily European clothing, although they retained their hairstyles, paint, and tattooing.

The basic Indian fashion included clothing, paint, tattoos, jewelry, and hair ornaments. Men wore the breechclout, leggings, moccasins, and mantle or matchcoat, along with belts, garters, and wampum collars. They had tattoos that indicated their war ranks, they slit the cartilage of their ears and ornamented it, and they wore paint as frequently as possible, in addition to painting for specific dances or for going to war. They wore feathers on their heads. Women wore their traditional knee-length skirts, leggings, moccasins, and mantles or matchcoats made of leather, cloth, and feathers. Both men and women wore garments decorated with porcupine quills, paint, beadwork, bells, thimbles, tin cones, turkey spurs, and deer hooves. Women tanned hides, produced cloth, made garters and sashes, and worked in feathers, shell, and possibly metal. All of these items and their decorations will be covered in the individual chapters to follow.

Long before the eighteenth century, Cherokees had been trading for items that they incorporated into their appearance. Ten thousand years ago, Chero-

31

"The Three Cherokees, came over from the head of the River Savanna to London, 1762. Their interpreter that was Poisoned." 8 ½ inches x 11 ¼ inches. Courtesy of the Museum of the Cherokee Indian collection. The interpreter, William Shorey, was not poisoned. He died on board ship before reaching England, of pneumonia.

Detail from powder horn ca. 1775 is the only known image of a Cherokee woman from the 1700s, and she is standing next to four Cherokee men doing the war dance. Her hair is pulled back and folded over in a bun and she has spots of red paint on their cheeks. She is wearing a short gown and a knee-length skirt decorated with ribbon or other trim in triangles reminiscent of Cherokee basket and pottery patterns. The skirt may be checked fabric cut on the diagonal, or the artist may be showing the texture of Cherokee twined cloth. Courtesy of John and Marva Warnock Collection.

kees traded for copper and pipestone from the Great Lakes region, marine shells from the Gulf of Mexico, and plants and shells from the Atlantic coast. In return, their soapstone bowls, sheets of mica, and feather capes traveled to the Ohio River valley, the Gulf Coast, and beyond. Trade in the eighteenth century expanded globally because of sailing technology and political events. British ships brought to America silk fabrics and silk ribbons from China, cotton printed fabrics from India, linen from Holland, silver ball and cone earbobs and silver breast buckles from Europe, and most importantly, guns and ammunition for the Indian trade. In return, Cherokees sent deerskins, ginseng, river-cane baskets, and corn to colonial capitol ports and on to Europe and China. The trade in Cherokee slaves, captured by the British, Spanish, French, and other American Indian tribes, lasted from 1540 through the 1720s.

The eighteenth century was a time when power was balanced between European nations and the Cherokees. At the beginning of the century, Cherokees retained all of their land and had a sizeable population, which far outnumbered the colonists. By the end of the century, Cherokees had lost much of their land, and their population was reduced by four smallpox epidemics. They were still one of the largest Indian nations in the Southeast (about the same size as the Creek confederacy), and they had about the same number of warriors as all the northern Iroquois nations combined.

This balance of trade and cultures has given rise to the term "middle ground," or "common ground." Historians now recognize that American Indians influenced Europeans as much as Europeans influenced them. Clothing styles reflect this mutual influence as well. Throughout this century, Cherokee people chose the trade items they preferred and used them in ways they determined.

While Cherokees and other tribes were adopting European materials and styles, Americans were adopting materials and clothing items from the tribes. The "well-dressed deerskins" were highly prized in Europe and America. Traditionally, skins were first scraped, and then tanned with a mixture comprising the brains of the animal. Hides were then cured with this mixture, softened, and finally smoked over an open fire. This processing results in soft, lightweight, durable leather that retains its size and shape even after becoming wet.

Deerskin prepared in this way by the Cherokees and other tribes had served as comfortable, functional clothing for millennia. By the eighteenth century, Europeans were using deerskin as well. Deerskin breeches were worn by soldiers and by men in general, and are still favored today by people who "ride to hounds"—foxhunting in the English tradition. Deerskin gloves were worn by men and women, and many books were covered with deerskin.

In addition to using these materials in European ways, some Europeans adopted the entire Indian dress: military units, men in the backcountry, and patriots on secret missions, like the Boston Tea Party. On a less genial note, some Americans dressed like Indians to attack their neighbors and blame it on natives.

The Indian dress developed as the century progressed, but it had a basic look for both men and women. Within this general appearance, there were differences between tribes. We cannot parse all of these differences, but we can know specifically what Cherokee people were wearing, based on written descriptions, artworks, archaeology, artifacts, and oral traditions. Cherokees, their clothing, and their appearance were described by a number of visitors including Henry Timberlake, William Bartram, James Adair, and William DeBrahm. Their descriptions generally agree and are supported by the observations of naturalists, including Andre Michaux and Mark Catesby, and visitors, such as Louis-Philippe,

King of France. In addition, the records of trade with South Carolina provide lists of items given as gifts and of prices set for particular trade items. Oral traditions describe the practices of the Cherokee people during the mid- to late 1700s, and were collected from elders by Daniel S. Butrick and John Howard Payne about 1830. Oral traditions from Cherokee people born about 1800 sometimes reach back to the stories of their grandparents from the 1700s and were collected by James Mooney in the 1880s. Missionaries during the Removal era (1820s–1840s) commented on eighteenth-century dress in a negative way and emphasized the progress toward civilization in terms of what Cherokees wore, and the extent to which it resembled European clothing.

Each of these visitors had his or her own point of view and purposes, but each provides a piece of the picture of Cherokees during this time. Timberlake, a soldier, lived with Ostenaco and his family in Tomotly in the Overhill Towns in 1762 and left behind a son he fathered with Ostenaco's daughter. His observations were clear and direct, and his purposes were diplomatic and military. Bartram was a Quaker who traveled throughout the Southeast as a botanist and spent several weeks with the Cherokees in the Middle Towns in 1776. His philosophy was that of the Enlightenment, and he saw that all American Indian customs had some reason behind them. He believed in the universal brotherhood of man, and his purposes were peaceful and scholarly. Adair, an Irishman, lived with the Chickasaws and the Cherokees from about 1735 to 1770. He had Chickasaw and Cherokee wives and children and was a trader as well as a political figure. His direct observations are clear and full of detail, but his purpose was to prove that the American Indians were part of the lost tribes of Israel. This Eurocentric idea enjoyed some popularity for several centuries but has since been disproved. DeBrahm, a German surveyor, was the architect of Fort Loudoun and spent several months with the Cherokees in the Overhill Towns. As an engineer, his observations are simple, direct, and focused on the natural world.

Here is what Lt. Henry Timberlake wrote:

The Cherokees are of a middle stature, of an olive color, tho' generally painted, and their skins stained with gunpowder, pricked into it in very pretty figures. The hair of their head is shaved, tho' many of the old people have it plucked out by the roots, except a patch on the hinder part of the head, about twice the bigness of a crown-piece, which is ornamented with beads, feathers, wampum, stained deer's hair, and suchlike baubles. The ears are slit and stretched to an enormous size, putting the person who undergoes the operation to incredible pain, being unable to lie on either side for near forty days. To remedy this, they generally slit but one at a time; so soon as the patient can bear it, they are wound round with wire to expand them, and are adorned with silver pendants and rings, which they likewise wear at the nose. This custom does not belong originally to the Cherokees, but to the Shawnese, or other northern nations.

They that can afford it wear a collar of wampum, which are beads cut out of clamshells, a silver breast plate, and bracelets on their arms and wrists of the same metal, a bit of cloth over their private parts, a shirt of the English make, a sort of cloth-boots, and mockasons which are shoes of a make peculiar to the Americas, ornamented with porcupine-quills; a large mantle or matchcoat thrown over all compleats their dress at home; but when they go to war they leave their trinkets behind, and mere necessaries serve them.

The women wear the hair of their head, which is so long that it generally reaches to the middle of their legs, and sometimes to the ground, club'd, and ornamented with ribbons of various colours; but, except their eyebrows, pluck it from all other parts of the body, especially the looser part of the sex. The rest of their dress is now become very much like the European; and, indeed, that of the men is greatly altered. The old people still remember and praise the ancient days, before they were acquainted with the whites, when they had but little dress, except a bit of skin about their middles, mockasons, a mantle of buffalo skin for the winter, and a lighter one of feathers for the summer. The women, particularly the half-breed, are remarkably well featured; and both men and women are streight and well-built, with small hands and feet. (Timberlake, 24–27)

Brass springs, obtained in trade, were used by Cherokee men and women in the eighteenth century to pluck hair from their heads, faces, and bodies. Courtesy of the Museum of the Cherokee Indian collection.

William Bartram described southeastern Indians in general:

The males of the Cherokees, Muscogulges, Siminoles, Chickasaws, Chactaws, and confederate tribes of the Creeks, are tall, erect, and moderately robust, their limbs well shaped, so as to generally form a perfect human figure; their features regular, and countenance open, dignified, and placid; yet the forehead and brow so formed as to strike you instantly with heroism and bravery; the eye though rather small, yet active and full of fire; the pupil always black, and the nose commonly inclining to the aquiline.

Their countenance and actions exhibit an air of magnanimity, superiority, and independence.

Their complexion of a reddish brown or copper colour; their hair long, lank, coarse, and black as a raven, and reflecting the like lustre at different exposures to the light. (1995, 111)

Bartram went on to describe Cherokees specifically:

The Cherokees are yet taller and more robust than the Muscogulges, and by far the largest race of men I have seen, their complexions brighter and somewhat of the olive cast, especially the adults; and some of their young women are nearly as fair and blooming as European women.

The women of the Cherokees are tall, slender, erect, and of a delicate frame, their features formed with perfect symmetry, their countenance cheerful and friendly, and they move with a becoming grace and dignity. (1995, 111)

Bartram was particularly impressed with his host at Watauga, just above Nikwasi, present-day Franklin, on the Little Tennessee River.

Iron scissors, eighteenth century, excavated in the Overhill towns. Courtesy of the Frank McClung Museum collection.

Two thimbles, eighteenth century, Overhill towns. Thread made from plant fibers was attached to these thimbles, presumably to attach them for decoration. Courtesy of the Frank McClung Museum collection.

This prince is the chief of Whatoga, a man universally beloved, and particularly esteemed by the whites for his pacific and equable disposition, and revered by all for his exemplary virtues, just, moderate, magnanimous, and intrepid.

He was tall and perfectly formed; his countenance cheerful and lofty and at the same time truly characteristic of the red men, that is, the brow ferocious and the eye active, piercing or fiery, as an eagle. He appeared to be about sixty years of age, yet upright and muscular, and his limbs active as youth. (1998, 223)

The Indian fashion was created by the Indian people themselves, beginning early in the century. Spinning, making cloth, sewing, embellishing with beads, and featherwork were already familiar to them. European-made needles, thread, scissors, and thimbles were items often traded to the Cherokees in the 1700s. Their quantity is confirmed by their regular appearance among archaeological artifacts. When a delegation of Cherokees visited Charleston to discuss and set prices for traders, South Carolina gave the following presents: "For each of the women now in town, 5 yards of Embossed Serge, some Beads, Needles, Thread, Ear Bobs, Cadiz, Gartering, Ribons, Scisors, Pea Buttons, Ivory Combs, and Trunkε" (McDowell 1970, 162).

Clothing terms (and their spelling) varied widely during the eighteenth century and are not equivalent to modern terms, so I will offer some explanation. Embossed serge was a lightweight wool printed with patterns. Cadiz, caddis, or caddice was a wool tape or ribbon used for decoration during this period. Gartering referred to a tape or braid about one inch wide, used to hold up stockings in European dress; hence the name. These were woven of wool, sometimes mixed with silk or linen, usually in bright colors. Some were plain, and some had patterns woven into them.

Timberlake said, regarding the creation of Cherokee clothing:

*[They are] great imitators of any thing they see done; and the curious
manner in which they dress skins, point arrows, make earthen vessels, and
basket-work, are proofs of their ingenuity, possessing them a long time before
the arrival of Europeans among them.*

*They have now learnt to sew, and the men as well as women, excepting
shirts, make all their own cloaths; the women, likewise, make very pretty
belts, and collars of beads and wampum, also belts and garters of worsted.
(Timberlake 2007, 32–33)*

Cherokee language includes many terms for clothing, cloth, and associated
items. These appear in the earliest Cherokee word lists, beginning in 1756. Clothing in general is referred to as *dihnawo*, the plural of *ahnawo*, the word for shirt
or cloth. Buttons are called *diktoli*, literally, his or her eyes. A handkerchief is
ayatsohi. The new item, ribbon, was called by an older word that refers to a
part in the hair, *agwelosdi*. Several terms for hides include *ganegaldi*, the skin
of an animal with hair on; *utso*, a raw hide; and *utsowodi*, a dressed deer hide.
(This was synonymous with moccasins.) The latter was the most valuable in the
deerskin trade. Words for sewing tools include *yvgi*, needle; *asti*, thread; *Iesusto*,
thimble; and *dilsdoyhdi*, scissors. Verb roots with their myriad conjugations exist
for weaving, dyeing, spinning, braiding, sewing, and making. (For a glossary of
Cherokee words related to clothing, see Appendix A.)

Cherokee delegations traveled to London to meet with the king of England in
1730, 1762, and 1765. The British public was very interested in their appearance
as well as their diplomatic missions. When Timberlake journeyed to London in
1762 with Ostenaco, Stalking Turkey, and Pigeon, crowds of thousands of people
turned out to see them at local pleasure gardens like Covent Garden. Their appearance was much remarked upon in the newspapers.

*On Thursday last arrived in this city [Salisbury, England] The Chief of the
Cherokee Indians in North America, attended by two of his chiefs. . . . They
are tall well made men, near six feet high, dressed with only a shirt, trowsers,
and a mantle about them; their faces are painted a copper colour, and their
heads are adorned with shells, feathers, ear-rings, and other trifling ornaments. (Timberlake 2007, 132n166)*

The *Gazetteer and London Daily Advertiser* described their clothing in detail
when they had an audience with King George III:

*The dress of Ostenaco was a very rich blue mantle covered with lace; on
his breast a silver gorget with His Majesty's arms engraved. The other two
Indians were in scarlet richly adorned with gold lace, and gorgets of plate on
their breasts. July 9; Annual Register for the Year 1762, Vol. 5:92. (Timberlake
2007, 146n208)*

Ostenaco and Stalking Turkey were painted by the foremost portrait painters
of the time, Sir Joshua Reynolds and Francis Parsons. (See color illustrations.) In

"A New Humorous Song, on the Cherokee Chiefs, Inscribed to the Ladies of Great Britain," by H. Howard, 1762. Figures are labeled the Stalking Turkey, the Pouting Pidgeon, and the Mankiller. This bawdy ballad broadsheet circulated during their visit to London. Courtesy of the British Library collection.

addition, they appeared in engravings in newspapers, and even in one of Hogarth's satirical engravings. They were the subject of a bawdy broadside ballad, illustrated with three figures copied from other publications. They were apparently very attractive to Englishwomen, because the broadside ballad begins: "Cherokee kisses are sweeter they say . . ." This satirical ballad was apparently written by a jealous Englishman and was quite popular; copies survive in the British Library.

Cherokees were frequently described as "well-made men." Today we would say they were muscular or athletic. The shirts made in the eighteenth century for Englishmen and other Europeans were shaped like a rectangle, to fit a basically rectangular torso. Cherokee men were broad shouldered and narrow waisted, then, as they are today. They did not fit well into the rectangular design of the eighteenth-century shirt, because when the shirts were made to accommodate their broad shoulders, they were too big at the waist. They solve this problem today as they did in the eighteenth century, by wearing finger-woven or leather belts.

The active lifestyle of the Cherokees, their diet, and their beliefs and traditions all contributed to their physique and attractive appearance. They danced nearly every night, played stickball games, played the chunkey game—they were running all day. They walked thirty miles to hunt deer and carried the deer home. DeBrahm observed that they were very good swimmers and that some children learned to swim before they could walk. Their next exercise was wrestling, jumping, throwing, and running, as well as hunting and shooting, with bows and arrows and with guns. The Cherokees' ability to run for long distances was often noted, with war parties traveling perhaps as much as a hundred miles a day. While British officers could beat Cherokees in sprints, the Cherokees always won when the distance was more than two hundred yards, because of their endurance. DeBrahm said: "An Indian once kept up, running a-foot, for three hours with the Author, who kept his Horse in a constant Gallop, from Keowe to Estetowe, and never left him" (108).

Cherokee people ate when they were hungry and not at set mealtimes. Cherokee food was roasted, boiled, and stewed but not fried. Wild greens ranged from

Warriors of AniKituhwa at Sequoyah Birthplace Museum, Great Island Festival. L to R: Kody Grant, Bullet Standingdeer. Photo by Barbara R. Duncan.

sochan to ramps to angelico in a yearly cycle. Nuts included hickory nuts, walnuts, chestnuts, and sometimes acorn flour. Wild game included venison, turkey, quail, buffalo, and bear meat. Fishing yielded brook trout, bass, and other fish (but catfish were not eaten). Wild or semicultivated fruits and berries included strawberries, raspberries, huckleberries, blackberries, gooseberries, pawpaws, persimmons, wild cherries, serviceberries, muscadine grapes, and more. Cherokee orchards yielded peaches and apples. Cherokee gardens provided several varieties each of traditional corn, beans, and squash as well as the plants introduced in the 1600s and early 1700s such as watermelons and sweet potatoes. Sunflower seeds, goosefoot, and wild potatoes were domesticated native plants that had been part of their diet for millennia. In addition, fasting for spiritual reasons was a regular part of life for adults. Ceremonies like the Green Corn Ceremony required four days of fasting before the feast. Men fasted four days before going to war, and their European companions, like James Adair, remarked on their tremendous self-discipline.

Compared to Europeans, Cherokees wore fewer items of clothing. Cherokee men going to war basically wore a breechclout and moccasins, with leggings for traveling. Cherokee women wore a knee-length skirt in warm weather, with or without a garment on their upper body. Their clothing was often decorated with materials from the natural world or those obtained through trade. As in many cultures around the world, functional objects also became beautiful objects.

This transformation of the functional into art applied to the body as well. Both Cherokee men and women had tattoos, as did most of the southeastern tribes. Europeans at this time had not experienced this tradition, and apparently had forgotten the practices of their tribal, Celtic ancestors, including the Britons, whose name meant "people of the designs," and their ancestors the Picts, whose name meant "painted people." The English word "tattoo" was adopted from the Tahitian and Samoan languages and was first used on the 1769 voyage of Captain James Cook to the South Pacific, coming into common usage later in the century.

The Cherokee word for tattoo was *udoweli*, plural *tsudoweli*. This word comes from the root word that means "marked" and was later used to describe writing. The Cherokee word for paint is *wodi*, and the origin of paint is described in the ancient myth of Stonecoat, a monster. When Stonecoat was defeated by Cherokee women, he was burned. As he burned he sang until midnight the songs used for medicine and healing; after midnight he sang songs that could be used to cause harm. In the morning, all that was left of his body was a lump of red paint, *wohodi*. When the medicine man used this to paint people, they became what they wished for: a good hunter, a strong warrior, or someone attractive to the opposite sex. This original paint was the red ochre. Colors of paint are distinguished by additional terms: *gvnige'i wodi* means black paint; *dalonige'i wodi* means yellow paint; and *wodige'i wodi* is the old term for red paint.

The red paint worn by the Cherokees and other southeastern tribes came from red ochre, a fairly common mineral. They also used kaolin to make white paint, and other minerals to make black paint and yellow paint. The oldest recorded use of red ochre in the Southeast comes from turtle-shell dance rattles dated to about four thousand years ago, in the historic Cherokee area. Cherokees and other tribes wore paint frequently, leading to their being described as "the red men" or "the red Indians." Cherokee face paint was often applied in individual designs and was worn by men and women. In the eighteenth century, vermilion was commonly traded to the Cherokees and used as paint. Vermilion comes from the naturally occurring mineral cinnabar, and contains amounts of mercury, which is toxic. In the 1790s, Louis-Philippe, a French visitor to the Cherokees, who later became King of France, remarked: "On the whole, vermilion is very stylish among them. . . . I even saw a few women who had painted their faces with vermilion, using it artfully and pleasingly" (Sturtevant 1978, 85, 90).

Using materials acquired from their environment and from trade and drawing on both traditions millennia old and new ideas, the Cherokees created their own Indian dress in the eighteenth century. The Cherokees' appearance, then as now, expresses their identity, their environment, and their creativity.

How to Make and Wear Red Paint

CAUTION #1: Do not take historical authenticity to the point of using vermilion or cinnabar, because they contain the toxic metal mercury.

CAUTION #2: Be careful not to inhale the dust of red ochre because it can irritate the lungs.

CAUTION #3: Among Muscogee people of the Southeast, women wore paint in the part of their hair and in two spots on their cheeks to indicate that they were available.

MATERIALS

Red ocher: This can be obtained in powdered form from art supply houses that provide pigments to artists who mix their own paint. One such supply house is Earth Pigments, www.earthpigments.com.

Bear grease: This was the traditional medium for body paint. It can be obtained from local hunters or by cooking a bear roast or other meat and rendering the fat. Refrigerate the roast, and when it is cool, remove the fat from the top of the liquid that cooked out.

Observe your local game laws.

Keep the bear oil refrigerated, and if it starts to smell rancid, throw it away. It should have a fairly sweet smell and taste. It was also used to season dried venison while traveling.

Sunflower oil or olive oil: These oils make excellent media as well. All are excellent skin conditioners. Sunflower oil and olive oil do not become rancid as quickly as bear grease does.

INSTRUCTIONS

1. Put a pinch of the powdered ochre in the palm of your hand.

2. Add about a teaspoon of bear grease or oil.

3. Mix together.

4. Apply to a test spot on your inner arm before applying to your face or large areas of your body.

5. Do not use if this irritates your skin or if you have an allergic reaction.

6. Use unscented baby wipes to easily remove paint from skin before showering.

7. Red paint on washable clothing can be removed by using a degreasing detergent such as Dawn dish soap.

A bit of cloth over their
private parts . . .
—Henry Timberlake,
  Chota, 1762

3 *Breechclout or Flap*

Cherokee breechclout
names
breechclouts in other cultures
adoption by Europeans
materials
stroud cloth
decorations
how to make and wear

When the Warriors of AniKituhwa decided to wear breechclouts, several were fully committed to this traditional garment. Others thought about wearing a bathing suit underneath, but finally they all decided to wear it in the traditional way. They find it comfortable and modest, and they wear it proudly.

They are the first Cherokee men in more than a hundred and fifty years to wear breechclouts. It's not surprising, then, that hardly anyone remembers this piece of traditional clothing. Few oral traditions have been passed down about this garment, with perhaps one exception. When Lloyd Sequoyah, a member of the Eastern Band of Cherokee Indians, talked with Ray Fogelson, an anthropologist, in the early 1960s, Lloyd would begin a story by saying, "A long time ago, when the Indians wore diapers . . ." Lloyd was being humorous, but he was also referencing the breechclout.

The Cherokee word for breechclout is *diseldi*, and the word for the belt that holds it up is *adadlosdi* (in the Overhill dialect) and *adatsosdi* (in the Middle, Kituhwa dialect). This word for belt is used today, but the word for breechclout was last recorded in North Carolina in the 1880s. In the 1700s, Europeans used various words to refer to this garment: flap, britch clout, brick clout, breechclout. The word "clout" is from the British dialect and referred to a small piece of cloth or leather.

Many indigenous people of North and South America wore a similar garment of leather or cloth, plain or decorated, during the eighteenth century. Aztec, Mayan, and Incan people are depicted in artworks wearing this garment, often decorated. Among the Plains Indians, Apaches, and others, this comfortable, functional garment was worn through the late nineteenth century. Today, some indigenous people of the Amazon region still wear a lightweight version of the breechclout.

42

Warriors of AniKituhwa wearing breechclouts, in front of Swain County Courthouse, Bryson City, former Cherokee town of Tuckaleechee. September 2, 2013, preparing to dance for the International Canoe Championship Opening Ceremonies. L to R: Sonny Ledford, Bullet Standingdeer, Will Tushka, Ty Oocumma, Bo Taylor, Daniel Tramper, Kody Grant, John Grant Jr., Karyl Franciewicz Miss Cherokee 2012. Photo by Barbara R. Duncan.

Many cultures have created and worn similar garments. Ancient Egyptians and Europeans before about 100 AD all wore a version of the breechclout. "Otzi the Iceman" died in the Alps about 5,300 years ago, on the borders of present-day Italy and Austria. His body was naturally mummified and his clothing preserved. He was wearing a leather breechclout and leggings made of long pieces of leather sewn together with sinew.

People in Africa, the South Pacific, and Asia traditionally wore and still wear versions of the breechclout. In the South Pacific, soft cloth made from pounded bark is often used. In Japan, the breechclout is called the *fundoshi*, and it is still part of Japanese traditional dress. The *fundoshi*, made of cotton or silk, is about fourteen inches wide and five to eight feet long. It is tied and knotted around the waist, and often forms a thong in back. Some kinds of martial arts, including sumo wrestling, are practiced in the *fundoshi*.

By the eighteenth century, Europeans had forgotten the breechclout in their clothing history, although some farmers and peasants still wore leather leggings to protect their legs while working in the woods and fields. They found the American Indian breechclout (and other traditional clothing) very different and curious, and "Indian dress" became a symbol for the continent and the different way of life.

Henry Timberlake describes Cherokee men wearing "a bit of cloth over their private parts." Bartram describes this garment as part of the wardrobe of the Cherokees, Creeks, and Choctaws.

The cloathing of their body is very simple and frugal. Sometimes a ruffled
shirt of fine linen, next the skin, and a flap, which covers their lower parts, this
garment somewhat resembles the ancient Roman breeches, or the kelt [kilt]

Breechclout reproduction made with navy saved-list stroud, silk ribbon, glass beads, and copper cones. Anonymous collection.

of the Highlanders; it usually consists of a piece of blue cloth, about eighteen inches wide. This they pass between their legs, and both ends being taken up and drawn through a belt round their waist, the ends fall down, one before, and the other behind, not quite to the knee; this flap is usually plaited and indented at the ends, and ornamented with beads, tinsel lace, &c. (1995, 121)

Indian men and women found breeches, trousers, and suspenders, the clothing of the European male of the 1700s, unmasculine, dysfunctional, and ugly. A German who wore suspenders among the Cherokees was given the name "Tied Arse," an epithet that was subsequently applied to all Germans (Adair, 70).

Conversely, some Europeans and Americans found the American Indian clothing to be very comfortable, even necessary, for living in the backcountry, for hunting, and for fighting. When materials for soldiers' uniforms became expensive and scarce during the French and Indian War, and even more so during the American Revolution, George Washington dressed himself and his men in what he called "Indian dress," reporting in 1758, "It is evident, Sold'rs in that trim are better able to carry their Provisions; are fitted for the active Service we must engage in; [and] less liable to sink under the fatiegues of a March." At least some of his men were wearing breechclouts, because in a letter that same year he ordered "stuff for breechclouts" to be charged to the public (Baumgarten, 69, 243). Numerous groups of Cherokees fought as allies with Washington, perhaps as many as three thousand men at different times in the war's campaigns (Wood).

When Cherokee men went to war, they wore only the breechclout, moccasins, and red paint. They carried their weapons and a bag, with a strap over one shoulder and a powder horn attached to it, to hold their shot, medicine, and other necessary items. Some took matchcoats for warmth and also laid them on the ground to sleep on. Some wore leggings if traveling through brush.

Early breechclouts among the Cherokees were made from leather or from cloth made of mulberry bark or other plant fibers. In addition, it appears from carvings on shell from the Mississippian period that men sometimes wore a teardrop-shaped flap in front with elaborate designs. This may have been part of the breechclout or an additional garment tied over it. Descriptions of ceremonies installing chiefs and spiritual leaders, collected in the 1700s, describe garments being tied on over breechclouts, as we might describe an apron today. These were made of leather dyed white, yellow, or red.

By the 1700s, breechclouts among the Cherokee had generally become a long rectangle made of leather or cloth. Leather was tanned using the brains of the animal and then held over a fire to absorb the smoke, a time-consuming process that created beautiful, soft, pliable leather. If it became wet, it dried to its original size and condition. Cherokees tanned and used the hides of deer, elk, bear, and groundhog. Each had different properties: elk hide is thicker than deer; groundhog is very tough. They also dyed leather black using walnut. White leather was used in ceremonies and may have been prepared using the mineral kaolin, which was available in the Cherokee area in large deposits. Their technology included using it to make white pots, white ceremonial vessels, white body paint, and in some towns white paint for the outside of their houses. Other accounts describe the use of yellow leather and red leather.

When cloth became available through the deerskin trade, about 1700, Cherokees started using cloth obtained in trade for breechclouts. They may have used linen, particularly in the summer, but they mainly used red or blue stroud cloth. A "List of the Prices of Goods for the Cherokee Trade" was negotiated between Cherokee leaders, traders, and the colony of South Carolina in 1751. They set the price of "2 yards strouds," meaning a piece of stroud cloth two yards long, at "3 Bucks or 6 Does." In comparison, the price of a gun was seven buckskins. This literal description of a deerskin comes down to us as slang for a dollar: a buck. (McDowell, 146)

This woolen cloth was called "stroud" because it was originally made in the town of Stroud, on the River Stroud in Gloucestershire, England. This town was famous for its cloth of the finest scarlet. Water used in the manufacturing process at Stroud passed through iron mines, and this may have contributed to the color; but recent analysis shows that the brilliant red color came from cochineal (Montgomery, 352–53). Cochineal is a dye made from insects native to Central and South America, so the cloth favored by Cherokees and other American Indian people was being dyed with material imported from America.

Cherokees and other American Indians also valued stroud cloth for its white stripe along the selvedge (or list) edge, where the cloth was fastened to a frame so that it could be dipped in the dye. This is sometimes called "saved-list stroud." As early as 1714, traders were writing to the manufacturers, saying that the American Indians were very particular about this edge on the cloth, and instructing manufacturers to add more stripes to make this cloth attractive for trade. Oconostota, a great warrior of the Cherokees, is pictured wearing a breechclout with one of these stripes on his French commission.

Later the term "stroud" came to be applied to all wool cloth of the same general weight, no matter where it was manufactured. Stroud is not as heavy as a

Oconostota, *Sgiagvsda egwa*, the great war leader, is depicted here in his French commission. He is wearing a shirt of traditional indigenous design, breechclout of saved-list stroud, garters without leggings, and moccasins. His face and head are painted and his ears appear to be slit. He carries a plain shot pouch and powder horn.

blanket, or duffel, as they were called in this period; but it is heavier than a modern woolen shirt, more closely resembling the weight of a modern wool blazer or coat.

The size of the eighteenth-century Cherokee breechclout, as described by Europeans, varies. Basically, it must be functional: wide enough to cover the man's parts but not so wide as to be bulky between the legs. It has to be long enough to have a flap hanging down in the front and back. Descriptions of width range from eighteen inches to nine inches, or half of an ell. (An ell is the same as a cubit, the length from a man's elbow to the tip of his middle finger, or about eighteen inches.) The length of the breechclout varies from person to person but is about forty-eight to fifty-four inches for a man, or the width of a piece of woolen cloth.

The Cherokees favored the colors red and blue. Some other tribes traded for black, yellow, or green cloth, but the colors consistently traded for and worn by the Cherokees were red and blue. This was so widely known and accepted that Henry Timberlake stated this as proof that he was being cheated on in a tailor's bill when the Cherokees were in London in 1762. He was billed for five yards of superfine, dove-gray cloth. He said that the person trying to cheat him was short-sighted because every one knows that two and three-quarter yards make a matchcoat and leggings, and five yards will not make two sets. He also said another color would have pleased them better, because they only wear "their favourite colors of red and blue" (75). In Cherokee color symbolism, red and blue represent the east and the north, respectively. Red was the color of power and success and was associated with war.

Decoration on breechclouts ranged from nonexistent to elaborate. Beadwork on existing clothing artifacts from the 1700s often includes an edging stitch as is still used today, with one bead upright next to one lying flat sewn along the edge.

Silk ribbons, *gwelosdi*, at least an inch wide were used for decoration, and these were given or traded to the Cherokees in a wide range of colors: yellow, green, red, blue, and so on. They were of plain silk, grosgrain silk, or moire silk. The "lace" that Bartram mentions is not like the lace we have today. It is a sturdy tape from seven-eighths of an inch to two inches wide, woven with figures in it. The most expensive kind, or "Tinsel-lace," was silver or gold and was used on hats and on British uniforms. In addition, Cherokees used bells, metal cones made of old brass kettles, tin cones filled with red-dyed deer hair, deer hooves, turkey spurs, and silver breast buckles (today called ring brooches) to decorate their breechclouts and leggings.

How to Make and Wear a Breechclout

MATERIALS

Leather: Brain-tanned buckskin (or elk, bear, groundhog) is what Cherokees used in the 1700s.

Modern deerskins will probably require that you sew two pieces together to get the necessary length.

Cloth: To replicate Cherokee hand-woven cloth, use organic cotton or hemp cloth in its natural color. It does not have to be heavy weight or burlap, because the Cherokee cloth was very fine.

To replicate stroud, use red or navy coating-weight wool or Melton wool.

Saved-list stroud is still manufactured today in India and by some artisans in the United States, and it is expensive.

Decoration: Silk ribbon still comes from China. Width should be seven-eighths of an inch to one and a quarter inches. It was plain, grosgrain, and even moire. Bias-woven silk ribbon can be purchased in specialty fabric shops but does not work well. A less expensive alternative is cotton or polyester grosgrain ribbon, plain or moire, in the same width. In the 1700s silk grosgrain ribbon had much the same appearance as this modern ribbon.

Bed lace can be purchased from hand weavers in America or a few English companies that create historical reproductions. It too should be at least one inch wide.

Cadiz or gartering was about one inch wide, with patterns woven in, sometimes in contrasting colors.

Cones of tin, silver, and brass can be bought from craft stores or suppliers of materials for creating powwow regalia.

Bells should be hawk bells or small round bells.

If using deer hooves or turkey spurs, be aware of state and federal game regulations.

Breast buckles are also called ring brooches and are becoming more widely available through makers of eighteenth-century trade silver.

INSTRUCTIONS

1. Cut a long rectangle of leather or cloth, about ten to twelve inches wide and fifty-four inches long. If using cloth, cut the rectangle from selvedge to selvedge, across the width of the material.

2. Decorate the outside of the breechclout on the ends, if you want.

3. When sewing on ribbon, you can put the rows of ribbon next to each other, creating a solid panel, or you can space them about an inch or so apart, according to your preference.

4. Put a belt around your waist.

5. Fold the breechclout in half to find the center.

6. Put the center part between your legs.

7. Bring the front end up toward your waist and tuck it under your belt. The end of the flap hangs outside the belt.

8. Bring the back end up toward your waist in back and tuck it under the belt. The end of the flap hangs outside the belt.

9. Adjust the breechclout so the front and back ends hang down evenly.

4 *Leggings*

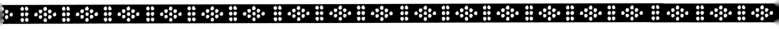

Both Cherokee men and women wore leggings. Men wore them along with a breechclout, and women wore them with a short, knee-length skirt. Leggings were attached to a belt or string around the waist by long strips that ran up the outside of the leg. The ties went up underneath any other garments, such as a shirt or skirt, and were tied to the belt or string around the waist. Leggings provided warmth and protection and were made of leather or cloth. They were made in two shapes—a rectangle or a trapezoid—and were often decorated. They were sewn to fit closely to the leg, and both men and women wore garters tied just below the knee to help secure the leggings in place. Artifacts and artworks show that in some cases additional stitching created a tailored fit that hugged the leg.

When Cherokees visited London with Henry Timberlake, a tailor presented a bill that Timberlake disputed. This dispute provides us with some good information about Cherokee clothing in 1762. Timberlake argued that the Cherokees did not order forty pounds worth of stocks and stockings, because "They are a great deal wiser than to be fine in stockings among the briars, at the expence of their legs, which good leggons keep unscratched, and a great deal warmer" (75). Clearly, leggings were practical wear. He further disputes the bill for five yards of super-fine dove-gray cloth at a guinea a yard, saying, as if everyone knew these facts, "Two yards and three-quarters make a match-coat and leggons, five yards will not make two; a coarser cloth would have suited . . . and another colour would have pleased them much better . . . their favourite colours of red and blue" (75). They preferred the heavy stroud cloth that was commonly traded over a lighter wool, and in this cloth, red and blue were their favorite colors. Blue stroud was what we would call navy today.

These details are supported by other descriptions, including the list of presents for the Cherokees from General Amherst in 1759. By this time, the British

leggings

materials

terms

adoption by Europeans

symbol of America

side seams

how to make and wear

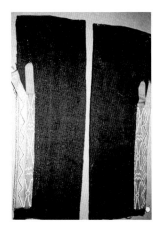

Rectangular leggings from 1700s, wool cloth, silk ribbon, glass beads. These leggings are probably not Cherokee because their color is green, or possibly originally black. They are described as simply North American, with no tribal affiliation. Photo by Shapiro Stanislav. Courtesy of the Peter the Great Museum of Anthropology and Ethnography (Kunstkamera) of the Russian Academy of Sciences collection, 1901-3A and 1901-3B.

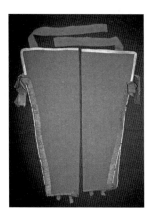

Trapezoidal leggings, ca. 1790, wool cloth, silk ribbon, glass beads. Courtesy of the National Museum of the American Indian collection.

knew quite well what articles of clothing and trade their Indian allies preferred. They sought to offer the tribes they allied with cloth in their favorite colors, and they crafted their promises of gifts carefully to ensure as much Cherokee participation as possible during this crucial year of the French and Indian War, when Cherokees were much needed as allies. Amherst specified that each man coming to fight alongside the British would receive two and five-eighths yards of navy stroud for a match coat and leggings, as well as six yards each of green ribbon and yellow ribbon to trim the leggings, along with other gifts of guns, powder, and ammunition (Mays, 74–77).

According to traveling botanist William Bartram, the Cherokees' and Creeks' leggings were "ornamented with lace, beads, silver bells &c." (Bartram, 121). Lace in the eighteenth century referred to ribbon or decorative tape, not the openwork weaving we think of today.

Other tribes also wore leggings in the eighteenth century. Adair was describing the southeastern tribes in general when he wrote:

> The men wear, for ornament, and for the conveniencies of hunting, thin deer-skin boots, well smoked, that reach so high up their thighs, as with their jackets to secure them from the brambles and braky thickets. They sew them about five inches from the edge, which are formed into tossels [tassels] to which they fasten fawns trotters, and small pieces of tinkling metal, or wild turkey-cock spurs. (Adair, 70)

Adair's description of a five-inch flap on the side is somewhat unusual. Other descriptions of the flap on the side seam state it as "a hand's width" or a few inches, which match more closely the portraits of Cherokees. Fringe was rare in the Southeast, perhaps because of the physical difficulty of walking through brambles in it. In artwork from the period, it appears more as a frayed edge than deliberate decoration, although it is difficult to tell from this distance in time. A few garments used in ceremonial contexts are described as fringed. Fringe was common among Plains tribes and became one of the stereotypes of American Indian clothing in the twentieth century. This stereotypical fringe was *not* part of the clothing the Cherokees of the eighteenth century were wearing.

A number of artworks from 1762 show Cherokee men wearing leggings. There are also written descriptions of Cherokees wearing leggings, but no known Cherokee leggings exist as artifacts from this period. A few artifacts from the eighteenth century, from other tribes, exist in museums. A few pairs of leggings from the Anishinabe (Chippewa) and other northeastern tribes exist in collections in the National Museum of the American Indian. Two very beautiful sets of leggings in European museums have no tribal attribution. One pair is made from leather decorated with dyed quillwork and metal cones with black-dyed deer hair. The other leggings are made from green wool decorated with silk ribbon and beads (Stephenson 2006, 13, 15).

The Cherokee word for a pair of leggings is *dilsgvlatvli*, according to Cherokee speakers in the 1880s, when a few Cherokee elders still wore leggings in western North Carolina (Museum of the Cherokee Indian MS2536). The word for pants or

Cones, handmade from sheets of copper or brass, possibly repurposed from brass kettles. Eighteenth century, excavated from the Overhill towns. These were attached to leggings, breechclouts, and moccasins for decorations and to make a musical sound. Courtesy of the Frank McClung Museum collection.

Bells, obtained in trade, eighteenth century, excavated from Overhill towns. These were attached to leggings and moccasins as decorations and were valued for their musical sound. Courtesy of the Frank McClung Museum collection.

Brass bell, obtained in trade, eighteenth century, excavated from Overhill towns. Courtesy of the Frank McClung Museum collection.

breeches is *asulo.* (An early nineteenth-century Cherokee man was named "Shoe boots," *dasigiyagi,* which sounds like some of the English-language descriptions of leggings, but he was in fact fond of Hessian cavalry boots, the forerunners of today's cowboy boots.)

Europeans called leggings cloth boots, shoe boots, leather stockings, Indian breeches, Indian stockings, and Indian boots. They were recognized as part of the "Indian fashion," and they became a symbol for the differences between the Indian and the European cultures.

Farmers in Britain still wore leather leggings in the eighteenth century, as protection when working outdoors. They wore a thigh-length or knee-length smocked shirt with these. European men commonly wore leggings and breechclouts until about 100 AD, or about the fall of the Roman Empire. The clothing of Otzi the Iceman, who died about 5300 years ago in the Alps, included leather leggings sewn up the side with sinew. By the eighteenth century, however, Indian leggings seemed like an exotic item of dress to Europeans. Visitors like Timberlake, Bartram, and Adair describe them in some detail.

This comfortable and functional garment had been part of the southeastern tradition for many centuries. New materials for construction and decoration were adopted in the 1700s, but leggings appeared and functioned as they had in the past. They were significant garments in the Indian fashion.

Most American Indian people found breeches and trousers ridiculous and did not wear them, as noted in the chapter on breechclouts; more than a few Europeans and American colonists, however, adopted leggings. Europeans in the backcountry of America, hunters, and military men had adopted much of the Indian fashion by the mid-1700s. George Washington, who valued the Cherokees as military allies and used them to teach tactics to his troops, adopted it for himself and his men during the French and Indian War:

In May 1758, he sent to Philadelphia for "One thousand pairs of Indian stockings, (leggings), the better to equip my men for the woods." Almost twenty years later, during the American Revolution, Washington again chose "Indian Boots, or Leggins" instead of stockings, explaining that they were warmer, wore longer, and gave the men a more uniform appearance. (Baumgarten, 68)

European cloth for uniforms was expensive and in short supply, and stockings and knee breeches were impractical. Washington himself stated:

Were I left to pursue my own inclinations, I wou'd not only order the Men to adopt the Indian dress, but cause the Officers to do it also, and be the first to set the example myself. . . . It is evident, Sold'rs in that trim are better able to carry their Provisions; are fitted for the active Service we must engage in; and less liable to sink under the fatiegues of a March. (Baumgarten, 68–69)

Washington was not the only American to favor Indian dress. The Overmountain Men, who fought at Kings Mountain during the Revolutionary War, the men in the Boston Tea Party, and men in the backcountry of South Carolina and Virginia all adopted this dress. It was practical in the mountains and countryside, but it also symbolized their difference from the British in Europe. As such, Indian dress became a symbol of America.

This style of dress continued into the nineteenth century. In the early 1820s, David "Davy" Crockett became a legislator from Tennessee. He enhanced his backwoods reputation by wearing leggings, moccasins, and hunting shirts in Congress and on speaking tours.

At the same time, James Fenimore Cooper began publishing novels about eighteenth-century America. *Leatherstocking Tales* was the title of his popular series of novels, featuring a hero who wore leather leggings and was friends with a Delaware chief. *The Last of the Mohicans*, published in 1826, was one of the most popular novels of the nineteenth century and featured a similar hero, who wore American Indian clothing, was comfortable in the back country of eighteenth-century America, and was friends with Mohican people. Cooper's novel became popular once again at the end of the twentieth century through a movie of the same name (coincidentally filmed in some of the original Cherokee territory in western North Carolina, with a Cherokee actor, Wes Studi, in a leading role).

During the 1700s, the seam of the legging was on the side of the leg. This was the predominant style of the eighteenth century according to all the evidence: artwork from the period, descriptions of southeastern people, and the few artifacts that exist in museums. After about 1800, styles changed, and by 1820, some leggings were being made with the seam in the front.

One artwork that depicts Cherokees in 1762 has caused some controversy in this area. The lithograph of "The Three Cherokees Come Over From the Head of the River Savannah" shows the center figure wearing leggings that have a line down the center of the leg. I contend that this is decoration, because on the

"Austenaco, Great Warriour, Commander in Chief of the Cherokee Nation." *Royal Magazine* 7 (July 1762): 16. Trim on the leggings extends from the side flaps across the ankles. Courtesy of the William Sturtevant collection.

"Habit of Cunne Shote, a Cherokee Chief / Cunne Shote, Chef des Chiroquois." From Thomas Jeffreys, *A collection of the dresses . . .* , vol. 4, 1772. He appears to be wearing breeches over side-seam leggings. This is not depicted or described anywhere else. Courtesy of the William Sturtevant collection.

portion of the legging above his knee you can see a side flap sticking out that is the right size, position, and proportion for side-seam leggings. It is worth noting that the artist does not render seams in any position on the leggings of the other two figures, so clearly he has taken some artistic license, and the center line may have been added for effect. (See illustration in chapter 2 of the 1762 lithograph.)

Four other engravings from this visit clearly show side seams on the leggings. The ballad broadside does as well, although this seems to have been copied from the other engravings. These are the only artworks from this visit that show the full figures of the men.

Today, the Warriors of AniKituhwa wear leggings in cloth and leather, plain and decorated, for dancing and as part of their traditional dress. They have added quillwork, silk ribbon, beadwork, and bells as decoration. The young women representing the Eastern Band of Cherokee Indians have adopted eighteenth-century traditional dress for the Miss Cherokee pageants. They wear leggings with wrap skirts, decorated in many ways. Some have used thimbles, bells, and glass wampum for decoration. In the summertime, however, for comfort, they wear wrap skirts and shifts without leggings, just like the Cherokee women William Bartram encountered in Cowee in May 1776.

How to Make Leggings for Men or Women

MATERIALS

Leather: Brain-tanned, smoked buckskin (or elk, bear, groundhog) was what Cherokees used in the 1700s. It was a natural, light-tan color or was dyed black with walnut.

Cloth: About five-eighths to three-quarters of a yard, depending on size.

To replicate stroud, use red or navy coating-weight wool or Melton wool.

Saved-list stroud is still manufactured today in India, or is hand-dyed in small lots, but is expensive.

If you are allergic to wool, you can substitute heavy canvas or polyester moleskin to get the look of trade cloth. You can also line the leggings with cotton, polyester, or silk fabric. Lightweight fabrics are not appropriate.

Decoration: Silk ribbon still comes from China. Width should be seven-eighths of an inch to one and a quarter inches. It was plain ribbon, or moire ribbon, or grosgrain ribbon. Bias-woven silk ribbon can be purchased in specialty fabric shops but does not work well. A less expensive alternative is cotton or polyester grosgrain ribbon, plain or moire, in the same width. In the 1700s silk grosgrain ribbon had much the same appearance as this modern ribbon.

Bed lace can be purchased from hand weavers in America or from a few English companies. It too should be about one inch wide.

During the eighteenth century, Cherokees traded for "gartering," which would have been a woven tape about one inch wide, in solid colors or patterns.

Cones of tin, silver, and brass can be bought from craft stores or suppliers of materials for creating powwow regalia.

Bells should be hawk bells or small round bells.

If using deer hooves or turkey spurs, be aware of state and federal game regulations.

Breast buckles are also called ring brooches and are becoming more widely available through makers of eighteenth-century trade silver.

Beadwork from the eighteenth century featured lines of single white beads in geometric design, and beads were also used for edging.

MEASURING FOR LEGGINGS

1. Measure the inside of your leg from the middle of your ankle to the middle of your thigh.

2. This is the length of your legging. In the eighteenth century, leggings reached to a hand's breadth above the knee or to mid-thigh.

3. Measure around your thigh at the point where your legging stops. This is the width of the top of your legging.

4. Make a loop of your tape measure and see if you can put your foot through it. For most people this is about ten inches. This is the width of the bottom of your legging.

5. Decide what decoration you are going to put on the side of your legging: how many strips of ribbon or trim, and what distance between them. Measure the total width of the trim. This will equal the width of the side flap.

CUTTING OUT THE LEGGINGS

You can draw directly on the cloth or use newspaper or paper to make a pattern first.

1. Fold your material along the width so that the grain of the cloth goes across the leggings and the selvedge is at the top of the leggings.

2. Using chalk or a pencil, measure length of your legging along the fold.

3. Measure HALF of the measurement of the top of your legging along the doubled selvedge edge. (You are using HALF because the cloth is folded, and you measured all the way around your leg.)

4. Go to the bottom of the length of the legging and measure HALF of the width of the bottom of your legging. (Again, you are using HALF because the cloth is folded, and you measured all the way around your ankle.)

5. Using chalk or a pencil, connect the bottom and the top of the legging. This will form a slanted line.

6. Along the slanted line, measure out the width of your side flap. Make marks at the top, middle, and bottom. Draw another slanted line parallel to the first one and outside of the legging.

7. Cut out the legging. Repeat the process or use a pattern to cut out the second legging.

8. Along the straight edge of the fabric, either lengthwise or crosswise, cut four strips one inch wide and eighteen to twenty-four inches long (depending on your height). These will be the ties for your leggings.

SEWING THE LEGGINGS

NOTE: If you are hand sewing, you will be using a straight stitch with five to six stitches per inch. If your trim is heavy and stiff, use a backstitch in whatever size the materials will allow.

If you are machine sewing, you can use between six and eight stitches per inch.

1. Sew the decoration on the flap before sewing the legging together. This is easier. Use thread that matches the decoration.

2. If the ribbon or trim you have chosen is very stiff, you can apply it flush with the edge of the trade cloth. If you are using heavy, tightly woven wool, it will not ravel out.

3. If you are using silk ribbon or a trim that is flexible, you can make a finished edge like a blanket. Sew the ribbon to the wrong side of the legging with a quarter-inch seam. Turn and press. Sew the wide part to the front of the legging. You can miter the corners if you want.

4. At this point you are going to have a RIGHT legging and a LEFT legging, because the trim should be facing the front.

5. Lay your two leggings out on a table. The decoration will face front, and that will become your right or left legging. Now you can decorate the other one so the trim faces front.

6. When your leggings have the trim sewn on, fold each one so the edges match up and carefully sew a seam just inside the inside row of trim. Use thread that matches the cloth.

7. Try on the legging and make adjustments to fit your leg snugly. To adjust, don't rip out the first, straight seam; simply add another seam.

8. Sew the ties securely onto the two flaps at the very top, one on the front flap and one on the back flap.

9. Apply beadwork, bells, or other decoration.

WEARING THE LEGGINGS

1. First put on the belt that you will be tying the leggings to. For men, this will be the belt that holds up the breechclout. For women, this will be the drawstring of the wrap skirt.

2. Pull the leggings on.

3. Pull the straps up inside your shirt or skirt to reach your belt.

4. Attach the ties of the leggings by tying them around the belt or drawstring securely.

5. Tie garters around the leggings just below the knee.

*[Cherokee women's] dress is now
become very much like that of the
Europeans . . .*
—Henry Timberlake

5 *Skirts and Cherokee Cloth*

During the eighteenth century, Cherokee women wore clothing based on traditions that were centuries old, and they continued to make cloth, as they had for millennia. Cherokee women also used new materials from Europe, China, India, Scotland, and the colonies to make and decorate clothing—in both old and new styles. Some women selected items of European clothing to add to their wardrobes. A few adopted complete European dress, especially when they traveled to Williamsburg, Charleston, and Philadelphia, but even then they kept their native hairstyles and tattoos.

At the beginning of the 1700s, the main garment for Cherokee women was a rectangular wrap-around skirt that extended to about the knee or above. These skirts were made of various materials: leather, finely twined cloth made by Cherokee women, and fabric made from thin strips of mulberry root bark.

These skirts were made using the same pattern that Cherokee women had used for millennia: a rectangle of cloth reaching from waist to knee, wrapped lengthwise around the hips and secured with a drawstring at the waist. One surviving example in the archaeological record is described in chapter 1: a skirt found in a cave on Clifty Creek, Tennessee. This skirt measures twenty-six inches long, from waist to knee, and was made of nettle fibers (*Laportea canadensis*). It measures forty-six inches in length, wrapped around the hips, and has a drawstring woven into the waist. The archaeological record also shows knee-length skirts on statues of kneeling women from Mississippian period sites in northwestern Georgia, north-central Tennessee, and elsewhere. A series of clay figures dated to 1200 AD shows women wearing knee-length skirts. These are on display at the McClung Museum, University of Tennessee, in Knoxville.

By the end of the 1700s, women were also wearing wrap-around skirts made of a rectangle of stroud, ankle-length linen petticoats, and perhaps linen shifts as knee-length dresses. They used European materials to make skirts in their

skirts

worn alone

terms

deerskin skirts

mulberry bark basket weave skirt

skirts woven of indigenous cloth

traditional Cherokee cloth making

stroud wrap skirts

petticoats

dresses

how to make and wear the wrap skirt and petticoat

Skirt and leggings, reproduction of Native American woman's skirt from Swedish museum. Navy wool, silk ribbon, glass beads, silver brooches. Sewing by Nancy Maney and Johnnie Ruth Maney. Beadwork by Heather Swimmer Younce. Courtesy of the Bradley Welch collection.

Skirt and leggings sewed by Johnnie Ruth Maney and Nancy Maney for Dvdaya Swimmer. Red wool, silk ribbon. Shirt fabric is cotton, the Colonial Williamsburg reproduction of "India Chintz." Courtesy of the Collection of Micah Swimmer and Carrah Shawnee Swimmer.

traditional style. They also used European garments in their own way by wearing shifts as dresses. Some Cherokee women also wore the entirely European ankle-length petticoat as a skirt, as did European women.

People who visited the Cherokees described the women wearing wrap skirts and leggings, but no portraits exist, and no skirts have been preserved. One skirt from a native woman from this period, trimmed with silk ribbon and black and white cylindrical glass beads, exists in a collection in Europe. (See color illustrations.) Wrap skirts of other tribes from the nineteenth century can be found in the collection of the National Museum of the American Indian, the New York State Museum, and elsewhere. They are similar in that they are rectangles of wool with decorations of trim or beadwork.

Traditionally, before the eighteenth century, Cherokee women wore the knee-length skirt by itself, or with other garments, according to the weather and the occasion. If it was cool, they added a mantle of leather, cloth, or feathers over their left shoulder. They also wore leggings, garters, and moccasins.

The tradition of wearing skirts as their only garment persisted as least as late as 1788, if not longer. French botanist Andre Michaux, when traveling through the mountains where the present-day states of South Carolina, North Carolina, and Georgia intersect, near present-day Lake Jocassee, was hospitably entertained by a Cherokee town headman whose mother-in-law and two teenaged daughters were wearing only skirts.

> I looked for an interpreter and a Cherokee Indian to go into the mountains inhabited by that nation.
>
> On December 6, 1788, I left for the mountains, and I slept with my guide in an Indian village. The chief of the village greeted us courteously. He told us that his son, who was to return from the hunt that very evening, would lead us into the high hills to the sources of the Kiwi [Keowee]. But he did not return and this old man, who appeared to be about 70, offered to accompany me. This man had been born in a village near the sources of that river, he knew the mountains perfectly, and I hoped that his son would not return. For supper he had us served fresh cooked deer meat and bread of corn meal mixed with sweet potatoes (Convolvulus batata). I ate with my guide who served me as interpreter since he knew how to speak Indian. The chief ate with his wife on another bench. Then the mother of his wife and his two daughters, the one married and the younger one about 14 or 15, sat down around the pot in which they cooked the meat. These ladies were naked to the waist, each having no other garments than a single skirt. (Michaux, 47)

When cloth and English shirts were introduced through trade, about 1700, Cherokee women began wearing an English shirt over their traditional knee-length skirt. They also developed their own style of shirt that observers compared to a sleeveless waistcoat or a short jacket with sleeves. (See illustrations in chapter 6.)

Compared to European women of the 1700s, Cherokee women wore fewer layers of garments. Proper dress for a European woman required many layers of clothing. The minimum number of garments included: a shift, stays, an under-petticoat, pockets tied around the waist, an over-petticoat, a gown, and often a kerchief around the neck covering the bosom. Custom dictated that middle-class women, lower-class women, and slaves also wore these garments, although instead of a gown, they might wear a "short gown" (what we might call a waist-length jacket) and shawl tied around the shoulders. Omission of any of these garments was considered scandalous, although women of the working class might roll up their sleeves and hike up their skirt hems as needed. The stays were a kind of corset that extended from the hips to the chest, with bone strips inside them for shape, and they were laced tightly. A woman who did not wear stays, no matter her class, was called a "loose" woman, with the same moral connotation that has come down to us today.

Because of the extreme differences in the meaning of clothing, the style of Cherokee women's dress was not adopted or copied by people in European culture, where women's breasts were not completely exposed. Europeans did adopt materials for clothing from Cherokee culture, however, the most popular being deerskins, which were used for gloves for men and women, breeches for men, book covers, military clothing, and more.

Cherokee women and girls wore only knee-length skirts in warm weather throughout the Southeast. Paintings and other historical documents from visitors to the region confirm this as a common style. Artworks include those by DeMoyne in Florida (1564), John White on the coast of Virginia (1585), DuPratz in Louisiana (1758), and DeBatz among the Choctaw, Natchez, and Creeks (about 1735).

Adair, who lived with Chickasaws and Cherokees from about 1735 to 1770, said: "The women's dress consists only in a broad softened skin, or several small skins, which they wrap and tye around their waist, reaching a little below the knees; in cold weather, they wrap themselves in the softened skin of buffalo calves, with the wintry shagged wool inward" (69–70). The Cherokee word for skirt or petticoat in the eighteenth century, recorded in 1756 by DeBrahm and still in use today, is *asano*. Today Cherokees use it to refer to both skirts and dresses. The modern Cherokee word for petticoat, meaning the undergarment or slip, is *hawini asano*, or "under skirt."

The word "petticoat" in English has changed in meaning from the eighteenth century to today, when it refers to an undergarment. In the 1700s, the English referred to both undergarments and a skirt worn as an outer garment as a petticoat.

The term "petticoat" was also used among men of the eighteenth century, both Cherokee and European, to describe something demeaning to a man. The garment was the symbol of the lower status of European women. When the Cherokees and Creeks disagreed at a treaty meeting in Georgia, a Creek leader harangued Cherokee chiefs: "[He] asked them what right they had to give away their lands, calling them old women, and saying that they had long ago obliged them to wear the petticoat; a most humiliating and degrading stroke" (Bartram 1995, 112).

James Adair describes the Cherokees as exceptional among southeastern Indians in the freedom accorded Cherokee women to marry, divorce, and couple as they pleased, without punishment. The Cherokees' own descriptions of the Green Corn Ceremony say that at this time men and women married and remarried as they wished: "They have been a considerable while under petticoat-government, and allow their women full liberty" (Adair, 181–82).

The traditional skirt in the Southeast was a length of cloth or leather tied around the waist. Cherokee technology for brain-tanning, smoking, and dyeing leather resulted in a soft pliable hide that was easy to sew and comfortable to wear. Its natural color was pale tan. Leather was also dyed black, white, and red, using walnut and other plant and mineral dyes, such as kaolin clay for white. Some ceremonial clothing used white leather and red leather, for the peace chief and war chief, respectively, while the spiritual leader or *uku* wore yellow. Cherokee elders told Payne and Butrick that in the old days, the wives of the priests wore a "petticoat of deerskin, as perfectly white as possible," reaching to the ankles, with a row of bells around the knees.

Another Cherokee technique for making skirts involved using strips of mulberry bark, most likely the red mulberry, *kuwa*. These were encouraged to grow near Cherokee towns, some of which, such as Keowee, were named for them. Cherokee elders who talked to Reverend Daniel Butrick and John Howard Payne about 1830, recalled the traditions of the past century: "Some Cherokee women made petticoats of mulberry root bark. They stripped the bark from the root, and then pealed strips from the inside. These would be a ¼ or ⅛ of an inch wide, and were then wove together like basket work; and being of a soft yellow colour, and of a soft pliable texture, they formed a handsome & comfortable garment" (Payne, vol. 1, 262).

Other traditional knee-length skirts were woven by Cherokee women from thread they had spun from plant fibers, the most common being nettle (*Laportea canadensis, Boehmeria cylindrica,* and *Urtica gracilis*), dogbane (*Apocynum cannabinum*) and mulberry (*Morus rubra*), processed into thread rather than the strips described above. These threads were used to create twined fabrics. Cherokee women wore mantles and skirts made from this cloth, and used native-made mulberry cloth as a base for some of their feather capes. They also used a length of cloth to tie their babies on their backs. The illustration of the town of Toqua painted in 1819, based on a drawing made by the Duc Du Montpensier in 1797, shows Cherokee women wearing short skirts and leggings, with babies tied on their backs. (See illustration in the introduction.)

I include a brief description of indigenous cloth-making in the eighteenth century for several reasons. First, it was common among the southeastern tribes and should be included in any discussion of their clothing. White skirts and cloaks were made out of mulberry fiber "practically everywhere" in the Southeast (Swanton 1946, 442). Further, this tradition has not been widely recognized and is little known, even today. Recent work by Penelope Drooker and Mary Spanos is only beginning to describe this widespread, significant tradition of indigenous cloth-making. Drooker's work includes sites in the original historical Cherokee territory, while Spanos' work focuses on Muscogean cloth-making during the Mississippian period in southwestern Alabama.

Also, it is important to correct the erroneous information that has been presented in many accounts, which state that American Indians did not have cloth until they began trading. This misinformation has been used to reinforce an ethnocentric and mistaken belief in the superiority of European goods and civilization.

This correction also helps us put in perspective the policies of the federal government in 1789 when it stated that American Indian women needed to learn to spin and weave (that is, with spinning wheels and looms) and the men needed to learn to farm. In fact Cherokee women, and most southeastern American Indian women, had been spinning, making yarn, producing cloth, and farming for thousands of years. The "Civilization Policy" had a hidden agenda, which was to encourage men to stop hunting so that tribes supposedly would not need the large tracts of land they had traditionally reserved for hunting.

Furthermore, the cloth created by Cherokee women was important within the culture in ways that exceeded its application in clothing. Flags made of red or white cloth flew over the council house to signal war or peace, respectively (Payne, vol. 2, 41; Timberlake 2007, 18–19). A piece of cloth was given to the priest to be used in certain ceremonies for individuals, as well as during the ceremonies conducted for the town at certain times of year (Payne, vol. 2, 24). According to the Payne manuscript, braided cords were also used to send messages regarding the time of meetings: "despatched his messenger . . . giving him a string of wild hemp, braided, having as many knots tied in it, as there were nights previous to the time of the meeting" (vol. 2, 205).

Cherokee plant materials that were spun and made into cloth included mulberry (*Morus rubra*), Indian hemp (*Apocynum* spp.), a native grass known as silkgrass in the early accounts and now identified as several species of milkweed (including *Asclepias syriaca*), slippery elm (*Ulmus rubra*) (Swanton 1946, 442), a milkweed species known as Butterfly weed (*Asclepias tuberosa*) (Witthoft, 25), and several species of nettle, including *Boehmeria cylindrica*, *Laportea canadensis*, and *Urtica gracilis* (Whitford, 12). See appendix F for more details about plants used by the Cherokees.

James Adair describes weaving in the eighteenth-century Southeast. He spent most of his time with the Cherokees and Chickasaws, so this may be a description of Cherokee weaving:

> Formerly, the Indians made very handsome carpets. They have a wild hemp that grows about six feet high, in open, rich, level lands, and which usually ripens in July. . . . When it is fit for use, they pull, steep, peel, and beat it; and the old women spin it off the distaffs, with wooden machines, having some clay on the middle of them, to hasten the motion. When the coarse thread is prepared, they put it into a frame about six feet square, and instead of a shuttle, they thrust through the thread with a long cane, having a large string through the web, which they shift at every second course of the thread. (411)

Adair is describing weaving technology that includes a weighted drop spindle for spinning, a fixed frame that stands upright in the ground, and the use of a shuttle.

Adair goes on to say that when the cloth was finished, they painted colorful images of birds, beasts and themselves "in their social and marital stations." This is almost exactly the same description as that given by Mark Catesby, who collected painted cloth from the Cherokees in 1724 to send to his patron in London, Sir Hans Sloane. Catesby describes this painted cloth as being made from mulberry bark and uses the term "carpet" and "apron" (Museum of the Cherokee Indian, Catesby 1724). Since mulberry and hemp were the most common materials used for cloth, perhaps the Cherokees painted on both of them, as well as using them for skirts and mantles.

Additional details of preparing the mulberry bark for spinning and weaving can be found in descriptions written by DuPratz, who lived with the Natchez in Louisiana in the early 1700s.

> *Many of the women wear cloaks of the bark of the mulberry-tree, or of the feathers of swans, turkies, or India ducks. The bark they take from young mulberry shoots that rise from the roots of trees that have been cut down; after it is dried in the sun they beat it to make all the woody part fall off, and they give the threads that remain a second beating, after which they bleach them by exposing them to the dew. When they are well whitened, they spin them about the coarseness of pack-thread, and weave them in the following manner. (344)*

He goes on to describe putting two stakes in the ground and "weaving" (possibly twining) between them. (Note the difference between weaving and twining. Weaving uses two sets of elements that "interlace," crossing over and under each other, usually perpendicular to each other. Twining encloses one or more elements within the twisting of two other elements around each other.)

Lye was also used in the process of breaking down plant material into useful fibers. According to John Reed Swanton, "When they have steeped these barks in water for eight days, they dry them in the sun for a very long time, and when they are dry beat them until they have changed into bast. Then they put them in lye and wash them three or four times until they are white. Then they spin them and make of them the cloth out of which they manufacture their clothing" (1911, 63).

Cherokee women were making cordage in 7500 BC and were making fabric certainly by 1000 BC, when it is found impressed on clay pots, if not earlier. They continued to make cloth throughout the eighteenth century. They used fibers from a variety of plants, mainly mulberry, nettles, and *apocynum* species (dogbane), all of which were commonly used in making fabric in other cultures around the world.

We must be cautious about European accounts that describe plants used in weaving as "hemp" or "Indian hemp." This was the term applied by Europeans to all plants used in making threads, cords, ropes, and cloth, because this (the Cannabis species, *Cannabinum* spp.) was the plant predominantly used in Europe for cord, rope, sails, and more. Most of the eighteenth-century Europeans who wrote down information were not botanists; they were traders, soldiers, diplomats, and spies, and they did not always make fine distinctions among plants used by American Indians. To further confuse the issue, one of the plant species the Cherokees and other tribes often used, *Apocynum cannabinum*, was given the common name of "Indian hemp." Research in the 1940s showed that artifacts identified as Cherokee were woven from the fibers of mulberry, nettles, and dogbane (Whitford).

The Cherokees harvested mulberry bark presumably in the spring, from the shoots springing up from roots where trees were cut down, and processed it by soaking it in water, beating it to separate out the useful fibers, drying it in the

Skirt decorated with thimbles, in the manner of the eighteenth century. Navy wool, silk ribbon, glass beads, metal thimbles. Sewed by Nancy Maney and Johnnie Ruth Maney. Beadwork and thimble decorations by Dawn Russell. Photo by Barbara R. Duncan. Courtesy of the Dawn Russell collection.

sun, beating it again, washing it in lye to bleach it, and then spinning threads of a desired thickness and quantity. As described in the eighteenth century, they then wove it on a loom made of posts fixed in the ground, using a shuttle of river cane. They may also have used posts in the ground as a frame to hold cloth while they twined it.

Cloth not only served a practical purpose but may have had symbolic meaning. In the festival for the first new moon of the year (also known as the great moon, the first full moon after the autumn equinox), the ceremonies included giving the priest a piece of new cloth.

No wonder, then, that Cherokee women were fascinated with linen from Holland, wool from England, cotton prints from India, silk handkerchiefs printed in Scotland, silk ribbon from China, osnaburg from Germany, and tapes and trims of all sorts manufactured around the world. Perhaps their traditional expertise in weaving gave them a greater appreciation of the new fabrics available to them. Certainly fabrics, ribbons, thread, needles, thimbles, and scissors, along with guns and ammunition, dominate every list of trade items and every trade agreement of the eighteenth century. Thimbles and scissors were found in the graves of Cherokee women in the Overhill towns. (See illustrations in chapter 2.) The first woolen stroud cloth was imported to America for the Indian trade in about 1705: "The women, since the time we first traded with them, wrap a fathom of the half breadth of trade cloth round their waist, and tie it with a leathern belt, which is commonly adorned with brass runners or buckles; but this sort of loose petticoat, reaches only to their hams, in order to shew their exquisitely fine proportioned limbs" (Adair 2005, 70). To interpret this statement it helps to know that a fathom is six feet or two yards. Half a breadth of trade cloth would be anywhere from twenty-seven to thirty-one inches and would reach

European women's work clothing. Short gown, America, 1800–1820, roller-printed cotton lined with linen. Acc# 1996-95. Petticoat, New England or Britain, 1770–1820, linen-wool, wool hem binding, linen waistband. Acc# 1991-444. Colonial Williamsburg Foundation. Museum Purchase.

from the waist to the knees of a Cherokee woman of average height. (The average height of Cherokee women at Toqua was 5′ 6″ according to an archaeological study, and this confirms the descriptions of Bartram and others that characterize Cherokee women as tall and Creek women as much shorter, about five feet or less.) Hams in the eighteenth century referred to the thighs. So Cherokee and other southeastern women substituted the woolen trade cloth for the traditional length of cloth fastened around the waist and reaching above the knee. They decorated this cloth with silk ribbon, trims, bells, thimbles, and beads. By the

1790s, Cherokee women's skirts were all made of European cloth, "red, blue, and embroidered" (Sturtevant, 200).

In addition to wearing their traditional wrap skirt in a variety of materials, Cherokee women during the eighteenth century wore the linen petticoat that was then a standard item of European dress. This garment was made of two pieces of cloth gathered or pleated at the waist and tied together at the side with strings. The petticoat was about ankle length.

During the eighteenth century, Cherokee women engaged actively in the deerskin trade, and traded corn and baskets for items like linen petticoats. In 1717 South Carolina set rates for the deerskin trade. The value of a linen petticoat was set at eighty-four bushels of corn (Museum of the Cherokee Indian exhibit). These petticoats were already made and traded to Cherokee women as ready-to-wear items and were often striped. The Cherokee word for striped linen in 1756 was *tsulaledi*.

By the 1750s and 1760s, however, petticoats no longer appeared in the trade agreements or lists of presents to the Cherokees. Striped linen does appear frequently, however, and Timberlake said the Cherokee women and men were skilled in sewing when he was there in 1762. Perhaps we can infer that by this time Cherokee women were sewing their own petticoats. There is, however, one mention, by John Stuart, Indian agent, of striped flannel petticoats in the list of gifts to southeastern Indians during this later period. So we can see that this garment continued to be a trade item to some extent (Museum of the Cherokee Indian, Catesby). A discussion of skirts would not be complete without a brief mention of dresses. In the centuries before contact, Cherokee women also wore dresses. Feather dresses were fastened over one shoulder and reached to the knee. These were made by fastening feathers to cloth or tying them onto a net. These practices will be described in more detail in chapter 8.

Cherokee women may have worn one of European women's undergarments as a dress: the linen shift. This was a knee-length linen garment with a scoop neckline and three-quarter-length sleeves. European women wore it over their stays but underneath their petticoats and short gowns (a short jacket). Typically the neckline and lower sleeves of the shift extended beyond the outer garments. This would be considered a fairly modest dress today. When Bartram visited the town of Cowee in May of 1776, he describes being in the townhouse as the town prepared for the stickball game with speeches, music, and dancing. He says: "A company of girls, hand in hand, dressed in clean white robes and ornamented with beads, bracelets, and a profusion of gay ribbands, entering the door, immediately began to sing" (1998, 233).

Their "clean white robes" may have been made from mulberry bark cloth; or they may have been European linen shifts, repurposed as Cherokee robes. Many clothing items were worn in different ways from the European tradition, and this may have been one of items that was "Cherokeeized." The shift was an undergarment for colonial women, but Cherokee women may have adapted it as a summer dress. The French term for shift is "chemise," and the French undergarments typically had gathered sleeves.

Shift worn under European women's clothing. White linen tabby, silk marking stitches, linen thread. Europe, 1780–1810. Initials R. D. P. are worked in silk cross stitches at the neckline. Acc# 1983-234 Colonial Williamsburg Foundation. Museum Purchase.

One more type of skirt is worth mentioning, although it appears in only one description. Some Cherokee elders in the 1820s described an unusual type of skirt to Payne and Butrick. They said it was worn long ago. Since this is our only description of this garment, it may or may not be accurate. "The women wore petticoats made of wild hemp, wove or knit close down to the knees, and then a fringe extended to the ankles. Women of distinction had feathers curiously wrought into this fringe." These elders also described a skirt worn by the wives of priests: "A short gown [jacket] and petticoat, of deer skin, as perfectly white as possible. The petticoat came nearly to the ankles, with a row of bells round it, not on the bottom, but about as high up as the knees" (Payne, vol. 2, 20–21). This, too, is a garment that is described only once, with no other evidence.

Fringe was not commonly found in historical Cherokee clothing (1540–present). The skirt from Clifty Creek rock shelter, as described above, has loops at the bottom and a series of concentric loops along the side.

Today Cherokee women are revitalizing traditional clothing by wearing the skirt and dress styles of the eighteenth century. They are wearing linen petticoats, striped and plain. Miss Cherokee contestants are wearing wrap skirts made of wool decorated with beads, silk ribbon, bells, thimbles, and trade silver. When they found the wool skirts and leggings too hot for summer wear, they began making shifts in the patterned cotton common to the eighteenth century, perhaps reinventing the same garment that their great-great-great grandmothers did generations ago.

How to Make a Wrap Skirt

DESCRIPTION

The wrap skirt is a length of wool wide enough to wrap around the body one and a half times and long enough to reach from the waist to the knee. It was most commonly red or dark blue and was made from a length of stroud cloth, heavy wool cloth originally made in the town of Stroud, England, and used in the deerskin trade.

MATERIALS

Wool: Of a weight comparable to a medium to heavy blue blazer. Lighter than a blanket. Red and blue were the Cherokees' favorite eighteenth-century colors. If you are allergic to wool, you can line the skirt (and leggings). You can substitute another heavy cloth that holds its shape: cotton canvas or polyester moleskin, which looks like suede.

Trim: Silk ribbon (*quelosti*) at least one inch, or more commonly one and a quarter inches, wide.

Ribbon can be plain, grosgrain, or moire. Favorite eighteenth-century Cherokee colors were yellow, green, red, and blue.

Other trims or "gartering" can be about one inch wide, woven in solids or multicolor, with raised patterns.

Metal cones with or without deer hair, bells, and thimbles can be sewn on the edge. Breast buckles (ring brooches) and trade silver were worn on the wrap skirt.

Beadwork can be sewn on the silk ribbon in patterns—commonly a single line of white beads was used for decoration. Sizes were usually 6–10.

Beadwork can be sewn on as an edging.

HOW IT WAS WORN

The wrap skirt was originally worn underneath a trade shirt or chemise that hung out over the skirt and was not tucked in. The skirt was made with a drawstring waist, or was belted under the shirt with a leather belt. For practical wear today, a drawstring waist is more reliable for holding the skirt up.

Put on your wrap skirt and adjust it so the excess wraps around, making two layers in front. Tie around your waist. Tie leggings to the string around your waist, bringing their ties underneath the skirt to the waist.

MEASURING FOR THE WRAP SKIRT

1. Measure around the hips. Multiply by 1.5. If your hips are forty inches, then your skirt lengthwise will be sixty inches. If you want to be very traditional, use two yards, cut in half lengthwise. The remainder of the two yards will make a pair of leggings with some cloth left over.

Hip measurement	Skirt lengthwise
36"	54"
38"	57"
40"	60"
42"	63"
44"	66"

2. Measure from your waist to just below the knee, or the length you want your skirt to be. For most women, this will fall in the range of twenty-four to thirty inches (half the width of the wool trade cloth is twenty-seven inches).

3. Add one inch to the waist-to-knee measurement for the drawstring casing.

CUTTING THE WRAP SKIRT

4. Cut a piece of wool cloth, red or blue, with the grain going lengthwise.

MAKING THE DRAWSTRING

5. Cut a length of twill tape, three-quarters of an inch wide. The length should equal your waist size times two plus twelve inches. This extra length allows you to wrap the ties twice around your waist, so that you can tie your leggings to them.

Waist measurement	Twill tape
26"	64"
28"	68"
30"	72"
32"	76"
34"	80"
36"	84"
38"	88"
40"	92"

6. Fold over one inch of cloth to make a casing for the drawstring. Fold it with the three-quarter-inch cotton twill tape inside. Fold it over to the WRONG side of the skirt. Before sewing, make sure your drawstring is far away from your seam so that it doesn't get caught. Sew it down and reinforce stitching at both ends.

DECORATE WITH RIBBON OR TRIM

7. Decorate with ribbon or trim sewn lengthwise. Ribbon should be at least one inch, and up to one and a quarter inches, wide.

8. Line up the pieces of trim next to each other to create a solid panel or space the pieces of trim a little ways apart, to your liking. When using heavy trim, you can sew it directly to the wool, flush with the hem, and the wool will not usually ravel.

9. If you are using lighter ribbon and want to make a finished edge, as in a blanket, sew the ribbon to the back of the wrap skirt close to the edge, using about six to ten straight stitches per inch. Sew about one quarter of an inch from the edge. Turn over and press. Sew to the front.

   Add additional rows of trim.

ADDING THE RIBBON BINDING

10. Add ribbon binding along the edge perpendicular to the lengthwise rows of ribbon. Go to the top of the last row of ribbon and allow several inches to hang down as decoration.

BEADWORK DECORATION

11. Beadwork (using round beads) was added to wrap skirts as decoration as edging and as single lines of geometric designs. Cylindrical beads were used as edging and in patterns.

Edging using round beads: place one bead lying flat alternating with one standing up. Or use two flat, two standing.

Geometric designs: Scrolls, triangles, and other designs were common in this period, in lines of single beads, usually white, about size 8. Cherokee patterns from stamped pottery or baskets were likely used.

Black and white cylindrical beads: Another style of beadwork used cylindrical black and white beads that imitated wampum. These can be used for edging or for designs. These were found on the only remaining native women's skirt from this time period.

How to Make an Eighteenth-Century Petticoat

MATERIALS FROM CHEROKEE HISTORICAL CLOTHING

Linen: Striped or plain, shades of blue and red with light backgrounds, about two yards.

Decoration: none is documented

About two yards of twill tape, one to two inches wide for waistband and ties. If you can't find twill tape, you can use wide bias tape.

MEASURING

1. Measure from your waist to mid-ankle or a little above. Add about one and a quarter inches for the hem. This is your length.

2. Measure around your waist.

3. Add thirty-two inches to your waist measurement. This is how much twill tape you will need.

CUTTING

4. Before sewing the linen, wash it in warm to hot water and dry on high to shrink it. After you have made your garment, wash it in cold water and dry on low temperature.

5. When cutting the linen, you must first pull a thread to find your line for cutting. This minimizes raveling.

6. Measure lengthwise on your cloth, using your personal measurement for length. Cut two pieces this length. The width of the cloth will be the width of your skirt before gathering. If you want your skirt to be slightly less full, you can trim your cloth to a thirty-six to forty-five-inch width, depending on your size. These skirts historically appeared very full.

SEWING

7. Gather the top of each piece of cloth with a gathering stitch.

8. Pull the gathers until each piece equals half of your waist measurement.

9. Fold the twill tape in half lengthwise to find the middle, and cut it half. Fold one piece in the middle again and pin this to the middle of the skirt front or back, so that the extended ends are even.

10. Pin the twill tape on the inside of the petticoat, adjusting gathers until they are even.

11. Sew the tape a quarter inch from the edge, on the wrong side of the skirt and the right side of the tape. Because the twill tape is finished, you don't need to turn it under to make a hem.

12. Turn the tape over, and sew a quarter inch from the edge on the right side of the petticoat and the right side of the tape.

13. Put the front and back (i.e., the wrong sides) of the petticoat together.

14. Sew up the side seams to within about six to eight inches of the waist.

15. Finish the side seams with a serger, a zig-zag stitch, or a whipstitch to minimize raveling of linen.

16. Turn under, to the wrong side, a small hem below the waist, and stitch, leaving an opening on each side. Pockets were not put in these skirts but worn on a belt around the waist. The pocket openings were covered by the shirt or a short gown.

17. Turn under a quarter inch of the hem at the very bottom. Press or stitch for a finished edge on the hem.

18. Turn under an inch at bottom for the hem of your petticoat and stitch by hand.

WEARING

This garment does not have a front or back. Pull on the petticoat and tie it at the sides.

Cherokee women wore a shirt, waistcoat, or short gown (jacket slightly longer than the waist) over the petticoat. If you want to ensure modesty, add some Velcro strips to the side openings to keep them closed.

They that can afford it . . . wear
a shirt of the English make . . .
—Henry Timberlake,
Chota, 1762

6 Shirts

Shirts were one of the most notable additions to the wardrobes of Cherokee men and women during the eighteenth century. Prior to that time, Cherokee men wore a traditional shirt made of deerskin or indigenous cloth. During the eighteenth century, Cherokee men and women adopted the English linen shirt, wearing it in their own way. They received these shirts as gifts, or paid for them as trade items, in various kinds of linen, checked, and printed fabrics, although white and natural beige were the most common varieties. Cherokee women began wearing shirts, short jackets, and shifts, and sewed them in plain and printed fabrics. Before and during this century, the most common garment for the upper half of the body was the mantle or matchcoat worn over one shoulder by Cherokee men and women alike (see chapter 7 for more details about the mantle). They did not wear the "hunting frock" or "hunting shirt" that was popular in the backcountry in the late eighteenth century and among re-enactors today. In the 1700s, Cherokees associated this garment with European-Americans who lived near their borders and often did not respect those borders. The Cherokees adopted hunting frocks and restyled them after 1800.

The ways Cherokees wore, created, adapted, purchased, and were given shirts in the 1700s inform our answers to many questions. How was diplomacy conducted and peace confirmed? How were Cherokee warriors paid for their assistance? How were the terms of trade negotiated? How did indigenous styles of shirts change with the introduction of a new item? When did Cherokee women begin making their own shirts and how did they change the European style to suit them? How did relationships with European countries and colonies change over the eighteenth century, and how did clothing symbolize those relationships? Everywhere we look, the answers to these questions involve shirts.

Cherokee elders in the early 1800s described the indigenous shirts of Cherokee men of the previous century thus: "The men wore a leather shirt, with sleeves

indigenous shirts for men
indigenous shirts
English shirts
washing
Cherokee language terms
gift giving and diplomacy
trade
shirts plain, ruffled, checked
prices
English shirts made by
    Cherokees
women's vests and short gowns
the Cherokee style
how to make and wear

Detail of Oconostota shirt from Commission.

coming down to the hips" (Payne, vol. 2, 178). This was a common style among southeastern tribes, as described by James Adair: "They formerly wore shirts, made of drest deer-skins, for their summer visiting dress" (69). This indigenous style of men's shirt may have resembled the one worn by Oconostota, the great Cherokee warrior, as depicted on his French commission of 1756.

It has a scoop neck, elbow-length sleeves, and falls below the waist. Cherokee women did not traditionally wear a shirt, but they sometimes wore a matchcoat over one shoulder or a feather cape.

A slightly different upper garment for men is described by another visitor to the Cherokees and southeastern tribes, Mark Catesby, artist and naturalist. Catesby wrote in 1743: "Their ordinary winter dress is a loose open waistcoat without sleeves, which is usually made of a Deer skin, wearing the hairy side inwards or outwards in proportion to the cold or warmth of the season" (Swanton 1946, 460).

The Cherokee word for shirt and for cloth is *ahnawo*. We have seen that Cherokee cloth dates back thousands of years. The language includes verbs relating to shirts and cloth that can be fully conjugated in all the persons and tenses, which shows that these words were not added to the language when English shirts were acquired but were words already in use. For comparison, we can look at the word "cow," *waca* in Cherokee, which is a borrowing of the Spanish word *vaca*. There is no V sound in Cherokee, so W is substituted. There are no other words in Cherokee language relating to cows, which the Cherokees saw first in 1540.

The words for cloth or shirt were clearly part of the language long before 1700. They may have referred primarily to cloth and were applied to shirts when they became part of the Cherokee wardrobe. DeBrahm records the use of *ahnawo* for shirt and *ahnawo utana* for matchcoat in 1756. The word for matchcoat is literally "Shirt it-grew-big" or "cloth it-grew-big." Since the matchcoat is more like a length of cloth than a big shirt, this could be another indication that cloth is the older meaning of this word. Cherokee words for cloth include:

ahnawo	cloth or shirt
dihnawo	lengths of cloth/shirts
uhnawo	Her/his cloth/shirt
tsuhnawo	Their cloths/shirts

Each of the following Cherokee words for clothing can be conjugated with past and present tenses, for all ten persons, making hundreds of words.

ahnawo'a	S/he's putting on a cloth/shirt
ahnawe'a	S/he's taking off a cloth/shirt
ahnawa'iyv'a	S/he's changing her/his cloth/shirt
uhnuwa	S/he's wearing a cloth/shirt

When the deerskin trade began, in the early 1700s, English shirts were a popular item. These had long, full sleeves, cuffs, and were approximately mid-thigh in length. Collars were either a rectangle that folded down or a small stand-up collar. Ruffles and lace on the shirts, as worn by gentlemen and by British offi-

Man's Shirt. Perez Richmond, America 1800–1820, tabby linen sewn with cotton thread. Typical length of 42.5 inches. Acc# 1953-967. Colonial Williamsburg Foundation. Museum Purchase.

Man's ruffled shirt, England or America, 1790–1820. White linen tabby with finer linen ruffle. The owner's initials W. H. H. are worked in silk cross stitch at the side vent. Acc# G1971-1552. Colonial Williamsburg Foundation. Anonymous gift.

cers, indicated that the wearer did not have to work with his hands. The shirts were made of linen and were sewn by hand, in a design made up of squares and rectangles. Accommodation to the curves of the human figure was achieved by the insertion of triangular gussets, rather than by cutting the cloth along curved lines as is common today. In this way, very little cloth was wasted.

An experienced tailor could, and still can, make one of these shirts by hand in one day. These shirts were made in large quantities in "factories" in England and Philadelphia and were shipped to Charleston, Williamsburg, and other points for "the Indian trade." The term "trade shirt" is a modern term, referring to any shirt of this period. In the 1700s they were simply called shirts.

As a side note, the first time I made one of these shirts, it took me more than three full days, and by the time I had finished it I would gladly have traded for the next one. Several Cherokee women, however, including Nancy Maney and Johnnie Ruth Maney, have become master tailors and now make these shirts quite speedily, as do the tailors at Colonial Williamsburg under Master Tailor Mark Hutter.

Both Cherokee men and women wore these shirts. They preferred to wear them as outer garments, while European men wore them tucked into their breeches or beneath their kilts. Shirts covered the breechclout and sometimes reached to the upper part of men's leggings. By the 1790s shirts were common among the Cherokees, as Louis-Philippe, King of France, a visitor to the Cherokees, remarked, "They all wear a shirt or tunic which is, I am told, washed fairly often. They bathe fairly often" (Sturtevant, 95). Andre Michaux, a French botanist, traveled among the Cherokees in the 1780s and commented, "A man's shirt and short petticoat form the dress of the women, who wear also gaiters [leggings] like the men" (Michaux, 263–64).

Bartram described how men among the Cherokee, Creeks, and other southeastern Indians wore the shirt, when he wrote in 1776: "The shirt hangs loose about the waist, like a frock, or split down before, resembling a gown, which

Warriors of AniKituhwa at Cowee, 2013. From L to R: Bo Taylor in striped shirt with fingerwoven belt; Hoss Tramper in white linen shirt with ruffles and leather belt; Sonny Ledford in white linen shirt with no ruffles and fingerwoven belt with beads; Jerry Wolfe, Beloved Man, in Museum of the Cherokee Indian shirt; Michell Hicks, Principal Chief, in ribbon shirt; Ty Oocumma in linen waistcoat; Daniel Tramper in white linen shirt, linen waistcoat, and fingerwoven belt; Bullet Standingdeer in checked shirt and fingerwoven belt. Photo by Barbara R. Duncan.

is sometimes wrapped close, and the waist encircled by a curious belt or sash" (1995, 122).

Shirts were always among the items given as gifts in the eighteenth century. Gift-giving was an essential part of diplomacy, extending far into the past for the Cherokees and other tribes. Gift-giving established a relationship and reflected the importance of reciprocity in Cherokee culture. Guns, powder, and ammunition were the most important gifts, but items for personal wear and for making clothing constituted the longest lists of items. Wampum, gorgets, silver armbands, beads, buttons, shirts, hats, clothing, many kinds of cloth, many kinds of ribbon and trim, needles, thread, thimbles, scissors, silk handkerchiefs, gilt trunks, and saddles were all common. The giving of strings of wampum and wampum belts was necessary for making treaties.

For examples of gifts and trade items given to the Cherokees specifically, see appendices C, D, and E. These lists of items tell us not only what the Cherokees had but what they preferred. Early in the eighteenth century, traders knew what colors, types of cloth, and items specific tribes liked and didn't like. For example, they knew that red and blue were the favorite Cherokee colors and that beads of purple wampum were more valuable than those of white for all tribes. Traders and military leaders considered this information essential to the success of their enterprises. They knew that the Cherokees and others were selective in what they would trade for and they acted accordingly, as retailers do today.

Gifts were given to delegations of Cherokees visiting colonial and European capitols; to delegations at treaty meetings; and to warriors when they went to fight as allies in the French and Indian War and when they returned from these military expeditions. Throughout the 1740s and 1750s, Cherokee delegations to Williamsburg were treated well, receiving presents and good hospitality, because colonial governors, especially Governor Dinwiddie, understood the importance of the Cherokee nation to both the deerskin trade and the military matters that were necessary for the security of the colony. These concerns applied to South Carolina as well. In 1762, Timberlake comments cynically that a large group of Cherokees accompanied him to Williamsburg because of the presents they would receive there: "I found it was the scent of presents, more than the desire of escorting me, that was the real motive of all this good-will" (49). He persuaded some of the party of 165 to turn back by giving them presents from the stores of a trader, Israel Christian, whom they met on the way. When Timberlake arrived in Williamsburg, about seventy-two Cherokees were with him: "On my arrival, I waited on the Governor, who seemed somewhat displeased with the number of Indians" (55).

This was the new Lieutenant Governor Francis Fauquier, who had modified Dinwiddie's generous policy of gift-giving, perhaps because the French and In- dian War and the Anglo-Cherokee War had by this time been resolved. Former Lieutenant Governor Robert Dinwiddie had correctly identified that American Indian allies were essential to British military success and treated them very well during his tenure from 1751 to 1758.

In the tradition of giving presents, shirts were always included, often in large numbers, along with large quantities of linen yardage for making shirts. When a large group of Cherokees, including twenty-two headmen, went to Charleston in 1751 to discuss the terms of peace, as well as new terms of trade, their presents were recorded. The 157 men in this group each received a shirt, hat, boots, and gun or hatchet. The women also received presents.

This meeting was typical of eighteenth-century treaty meetings between the Cherokees and the colonies. Both Virginia and South Carolina enacted laws reg- ulating trade specifically with the Cherokees, including the prices of goods, laws governing traders, and licenses of traders, as early as 1717, and continued to do so throughout the century. At this midpoint, 1751, the war between the Cherokees and the Creeks had just ended. Cherokees were feeling the loss of population following the smallpox epidemic of 1738. More and more settlers were coming into the backcountry, especially in upper South Carolina. Before talks began in Charleston in 1751, presents were distributed. The headman of "Eufassee" (possi- bly Hiwassee) was given the following: "For the Raven, a scarlet coat, Wastcoat and Breches, ruffled Shirt, gold-laced Hat, Shoes, Buckles, Buttons, Stockins and Gartring, Saddle, one of the best Guns, Cutlass, a Blanket and Knife, a Peice of stroud, 5 Yards of Callico, ten Yards of Embossed Serge." The same items were given to Moytoy of Great Tellico and "the Chotee King." The present of a scarlet coat, waistcoat, and breeches was sometimes given by colonial powers to the highest ranking American Indian leaders, and these were usually trimmed with gold "lace," a sturdy metallic trim about one inch wide. The coats were sometimes called "chief's coats." (See color illustration of Walker Calhoun.) The coats, waistcoats, and breeches were the same as those worn by European and colonial men and British soldiers, although sometimes the coat and waistcoat were not lined when given as gifts to American Indians. The hats refer to the tricorner hat popular at the time, and "laced hats" were trimmed with gold or silver trim, about an inch wide. Again, note that this is not the same as modern "lace." A piece of stroud was typically twenty to thirty yards long.

The Raven's son, Moytoy, was given "one of the best Coats out of the Publick Store, a white Shirt, a Gun, a Flag, Shoes and Stockins, Buckles and garters, a laced Hat, and 5 yards of embossed serge and a Commission" (McDowell 1958, 161–62).

The same items were given, with a few variations, to the Good Warrior of Estatoe; Caesar of Great Tellico; the Blind Warrior of Great Tellico; Chucheechee of Tusckaseegee; and Tosetee of Stekoe. The same was given to Skiagvsda of Keowee with "a saddle for his wife but none for himself." From this list it seems that the Lower Towns, Middle Towns, and Overhill Towns were all represented. In addition to the named men, nineteen "chiefs of an inferior rank" were each given a coat, gun, shirt, flax, hat, and boots. The chiefs were given additional presents to distribute to the 128 Cherokee men who were with the group: 64 guns and 64 hatchets. Each of the 128 men was also given "a Shirt, Hat, and Boots."

Out of the 157 Cherokee men in this delegation, each one received at minimum a shirt, hat, boots, and a gun or hatchet. The Charleston commissioners of trade gave ruffled shirts to only the three highest warriors. The Cherokee women with them also received presents, as noted elsewhere, but these did not include shirts. The governor in his concluding remarks said that more presents were given at this meeting than at any other, in the amount of twelve hundred weight of leather, which was equal to the skins of six hundred male deer or twelve hundred does.

By the time talks were concluded, articles had been agreed upon. According to the first:

> There should be a perpetual Peace and perfect good Understanding betwixt His Majesty King George's Subjects of South Carolina and the Nation of Indians called Cherokees, and all Disputes and all Differences, all Wrongs and Injuries whether of an old or more modern Date that have been committed by the Cherokee Nation, shall be forgiven and forgotten, shall never more be mentioned or thought of but buried in eternal Oblivion, except what follows, that is to say. (McDowell 1958, 188)

The articles agreed that settlement would be reached for missing and stolen deerskins and horses; that Cherokees whose horses were stolen would be compensated; that any white man or trader among them would not be robbed; that runaway slaves would be returned; that the Cherokees would prevent French and Northern Indians from coming among the settlements; that traders would be licensed to trade only in particular towns; that traders would not be permitted to carry rum; that traders would use equal weights and measures, and that the headman of each Cherokee town would also have a set of these weights and measures so as to be able to check on the traders; that Cherokees would sell their skins only in their own towns; that traders would not give credit to any Cherokee more than one year's hunt, or twenty-four weight of leather. The terms of trade were also set.

When Cherokees attempted to visit King George III in 1765, following the group taken by Timberlake in 1762, Edwin Montagu estimated the expense to Virginia. His list of presents to them included shirts. In addition to the expenses for their passage, provisions, lodging, coachman, and "To the captain for the use of his Cabin," the list of gifts included scarlet cloth, the making of mantles, vermilion, looking glasses, combs, Indian flannel, matchcoats, strouds, canvas, three pair silver bracelets, and eighteen shirts.

Like diplomatic emissaries and delegations, Cherokee war parties were given extensive presents, which represented their relationship as allies, provided supplies, and served as payment or incentive for fighting. In 1758, when the French and Indian War was escalating and the British desperately needed the Cherokees as allies, Colonel Byrd listed the presents taken from the stores of various traders and given by him to "The Great Warriour and His Gang." At this time the Cherokees had three thousand warriors in their nation, and their great war leader was Oconostota. They sent as many as six to eight hundred warriors at one time to assist the British in the field.

Between April 4 and May 2, 1758, at various locations supplied by various traders, weapons and supplies given as presents included: 105 guns, 2800 weight bullets, 825 pounds of lead, 1312 weight gunpowder, and some bags of flints. Hatchets, knives, and paint were also given.

Significant among these presents are shirts, cloth, trims, and other personal items. These included 64 shirts and 460 checked shirts. Gifts also included 748 yards of stroud cloth for breechclouts, matchcoats, and leggings. Cloth for making shirts was also given, more than 326 yards of linen in the form of oznaburgh and garlix. An additional 1,651 yards of striped, checked, and printed cloth was given. These amounts total 524 shirts and 2,725 yards of fabric. To understand the magnitude of these gifts, consider that placed lengthwise this amount of fabric would stretch more than a mile and a half. Presents also included more than two gross of decorative trims in the form of ribbon, cadiz, and gartering. This amounts to 288 pieces, each including many yards of trim. Some of the fabric had specific applications: "6 yards of Negro cloth for powder bags and 4 and 1/2 yards oznabrigs for shott baggs" (McDowell 1970, 456–58).

How many Cherokees would this outfit, however? If we estimate five hundred warriors at this meeting, then each man would receive a shirt. Only one in five would receive a gun. Each would receive about a yard and a half of stroud—not enough for a matchcoat and leggings. Each would receive about three yards of linen or printed fabric—enough for another shirt to be made at home, along

Checked or Check'd cloth typical of 1700s. Textile Sample Book by Benjamin and John Bower, Manchester England, 1771. Page size 8¼ inches x 4⅔ inches. Attached samples are fustian (heavy cotton). Most are blue and white. This book was sent to New York to market fabrics from England. Courtesy of the Colonial Williamsburg collection.

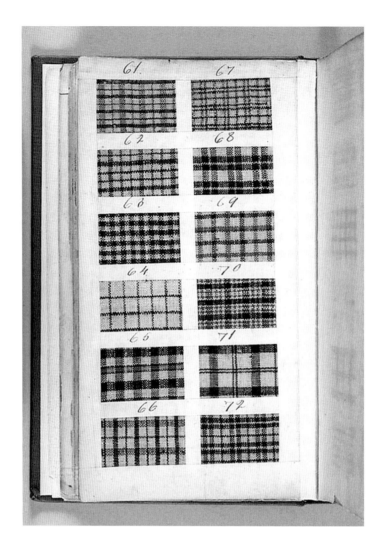

with some ribbon. Whether the amount of bullets, lead, and powder was adequate is not clear.

The words for cloth and trims varied in their use and spelling in the eighteenth century. See appendix B for a list of English terms found in Cherokee gift lists and trade agreements. Garlix was the most common form of linen used to make shirts and was white or unbleached. Osnaburg was unbleached and a little coarser than garlix. Checked linen was very popular in America for shirts. "Checked" in the 1700s referred to any design with perpendicular lines that crossed; some of the checked fabrics of the 1700s are known today as gingham, tattersall, and plaid.

In the negotiations of 1751, as discussed above, the leaders of Cherokee towns talked through an interpreter with Governor Glen from November 23 to November 28. In addition to the matters of alliance and trade described above, some negotiations on prices took place as well. Skiagunsta, the Warrior of Keowee, said, "When your Excellency talked the other Day about raising the Price to seven Weight of Leather for a Match-Coat, I was here, but I did not like to hear that as I had no Directions from my People to talk about it. But as I hear no more of it now I am very glad. A Match-Coat is now 6 Weight of Leather, but I want a Shirt to be lowered to three Weight." The Governor replied, "When Shirts are good they are worth four Weight, but when indifferent three. We don't raise the Price on them and I am surprised they should lower the Price now" (McDowell [1958] 193).

The prices set for shirts were:

A Garlix Shirt	2 Bucks or 4 Does [four weight]
Fine Rufel [ruffled] Shirts	4 Bucks or 8 Does [eight weight]

Prices set for shirts in July 1762, in the agreements following the Cherokee-Anglo War were as follows:

Shirt, a checked one	3 weight [1 buck and 1 doe skin]
Shirt, a white one	3 weight [1 buck and 1 doe skin]
(McDowell 1970, 568)	

But by November 1762, prices had gone up, at least at the Factory at Fort Prince George, Keowee.

Shirts, now sent,

white-plain a Peece	7 weight [3 bucks and 1 doe]
checked-plain a Peece	7 weight [3 bucks and 1 doe]
white-ruffled a Peece	9 weight [4 bucks and 1 doe]
checked-ruffled a Peece	8 weight [4 bucks]
(McDowell 1970, 576)	

Cherokee men wore the English shirt acquired through trade and as gifts, in plain white, unbleached, and checked linen. In addition, the Cherokees were giving shirts as gifts and were purchasing large quantities of fabrics. Any shirts made of these materials would have been constructed by the Cherokees themselves. These included linen, garlix, osnaburg, checked, striped, and printed linen and wool. In the list of prices for November 1762, white linen was one and a half weight per yard. If at least two and a half yards were required to make a shirt, then the material would have cost almost four weight of leather, about half the price of a ready-made shirt—a significant savings. Timberlake may have been wrong in his observation that they did not make their own shirts: "They have now learnt to sew, and the men as well as women, excepting shirts, make all their own cloaths" (33). As further evidence we have the inventory of John Vann when he purchased his stock to begin trading with the Cherokees in June 1764. This list includes three dozen shirts, but the many hundreds of yards of linen in his inventory far overshadow those thirty-six garments. Although the ready-made shirts continue to appear in all the lists of gifts and trade, it would seem that by this time Cherokees were also sewing a significant number of shirts. (See appendix E for Vann's license and complete inventory.)

Cherokee women wore English shirts but also made their own style of upper garment: "The women wore a skirt and short jacket, with leggings and moccasins, the jacket was fastened in front with silver broaches" (Kilpatrick 1966, 191). This description comes from Waunenauhi, the granddaughter of George Lowery,

Tonya Carroll, Miss Cherokee 2010, wears a sleeveless bodice of cotton print from Colonial Williamsburg reproduction collection. Linen skirt, fingerwoven belt, deerskin moccasins, white oak basket. In front of Tribal Council House, fall 2010. Photo by Bear Allison.

Short gown, block printed, England, 1775–1815, cotton, linen tape, acc# 1985-242. Colonial Williamsburg Foundation. Museum Purchase.

cousin of Sequoyah. She was recounting his descriptions of the eighteenth century. Her details are confirmed by William Bartram's description of the Cherokee women and Creek women in 1775: "They have no shirt or shift but a little shirt waistcoat, usually made of callico, or printed linen, or fine cloth, decorated with lace, beads, &c." (1995, 122).

Cherokee women may have adopted the short gown of European women or the waistcoat of European men, but it seems clear that by the second half of the eighteenth century they were wearing a garment on the upper body that was some kind of jacket, either with sleeves or without. Callico refers to cotton cloth from India that may have been plain, dyed, printed, or chintz. Note that its appearance is different from the tiny flowers of modern calico. When Waunenauhi says the jacket was fastened with silver broaches, she is most likely referring to the "breast buckles" or small round brooches used in Europe to fasten men's shirtfronts. These became popular as a trade item early in the century. When Bartram says these were decorated with lace, this refers to a solid or multicolored trim about an inch wide, woven in patterns, not modern lace. These trims were traded and sold in large quantities to the Cherokees. The upper garments worn by European women included a shift as an undergarment, with a "short gown" or "bed jacket" over it. It seems that Cherokee women adapted these for their own use and used new fabrics and trims along with traditional beads to create their own style.

Cherokees wore English shirts throughout the eighteenth century. The shirts were made of white linen with ruffles, plain white linen, checked linen, checked linen with ruffles, or striped linen. Men received them as presents at treaty negotiations and acquired them through trade for deerskins. They wore them in their own style, with breechclouts and leggings, and not at all when they went to war. Cherokee women wore English shirts as well, in their own style as an outer garment. In addition, they sewed shirts out of a wide variety of linen, both plain and printed, and possibly out of cotton and wool fabrics. Cherokee women further adapted English styles and materials by constructing short jackets and waistcoats for themselves out of plain, striped, and printed linen and wool fabrics, decorated in their own original way with beads and trims. The shirts were English, but the Cherokees remade them in their own Cherokee style.

How to Make and Wear the Cherokee Shirt of the Eighteenth Century

MATERIALS, PLAIN

Linen was the fabric of the eighteenth-century shirt and was usually plain. It could be fine white linen, medium-weight white linen, slightly coarser linen such as garlix bleached or unbleached, or a rougher more heavyweight linen such as osnaburgh with a tan or beige color.

If you substitute cotton or muslin the appearance will be slightly different because these fabrics do not have as much body, or stiffness.

If you add ruffles to a white linen shirt, these can be of lightweight handkerchief linen, also called cambric.

MATERIALS, CHECKED

The checks of checked linen were about a quarter inch wide and were woven in. Common colors were red and white, crimson and white, blue and white, green and white, and yellow and white. Other checked fabrics are those known as tattersall, gingham, and plaid—any pattern with lines that intersect perpendicularly.

MATERIALS, PRINTED

These include chintz or spriggy fabrics with blue or red flowers on a light background, white sprigs on a medium blue background, and red or blue flowers or sprigs on a light background. Some such fabric is still made in India today.

Reproduction fabrics are being produced by Colonial Williamsburg and by Den Haan & Wagenmakers in the Netherlands. Other reproductions and approximations are available from fabric manufacturers and in retail stores.

PATTERNS

Shirts can be made from scratch by tailoring to individual measurements. Patterns make this much easier. A number of companies—for example, J. P. Ryan, Kannik's Korner, Eagle View, and PeeGee's—offer historically accurate patterns for eighteenth-century men's shirts, jackets, and waistcoats and women's shifts and short gowns.

TIPS FOR CUTTING AND SEWING LINEN

First, shrink the fabric by washing in warm water and drying it on a warm setting. After you make the garment, always wash it in cold water and dry it on low heat or hang to dry.

When cutting linen, first pull a thread. Snip where you want to cut, then pull one thread in the direction of the cut. When you have pulled it out all the way across the fabric, cut carefully along the line it makes. This will minimize raveling.

When sewing linen, you must finish the seams or they will ravel. You can make French seams, serge the edges inside the garment, or zigzag stitch the edges inside the garment.

Shirts made by tailors were hemmed at the bottom. Some of the shirts made by Cherokees and other tribes were not hemmed. They were worn about hip-length.

How to Make and Wear the Cherokee Women's Shirt of the Eighteenth Century

This can be a plain, print, or checked linen shirt as described above. To imitate the waistcoat or short gown described by Bartram and others, use a pattern for an English bodice or short gown. Materials are the same as described above.

A large mantle or match-coat
thrown over all compleats their
dress at home; but when they go
to war they leave their trinkets
behind, and the mere necessaries
serve them.
—Henry Timberlake,
   Chota, 1762

7 *Mantles or Matchcoats*

For warmth, Cherokees wore tanned hides, cloth, or a mantle of feathers over one or both shoulders. These items of clothing were depicted in shell gorgets and stone carvings a thousand years before the eighteenth century. Feather mantles will be discussed in the next chapter.

When Henry Timberlake visited the Overhill Towns in 1762, he found that "the old people still remember and praise the ancient days, before they were acquainted with the whites, when they had but little dress, except a bit of skin about their middles, mockasons, a mantle of buffalo skin for the winter, and a lighter one of feathers for the summer" (27).

The buffalo skin mantles would have been very warm. Buffalo were native to the southern Appalachians. Cherokee elders further confirmed the tradition of wearing mantles, telling John Howard Payne that "their blankets were as now, only made of leather. These being belted round the waist, were brought over the left shoulder, and under the right arm, that is when hunting" (vol. 2, 178).

Southeastern people used the skins of buffalo, bear, elk, and deer for warmth, as mantles, and as bed coverings. They sewed rabbit skins together as well (Swanton 1946, 249–50). Some of these tanned hides were painted on the smooth side, as depicted in a drawing that appears to be a panther skin with the hair and tail left on, painted on the smooth surface worn on the inside. This was painted in Louisiana sometime between 1732 and 1752 by DeBatz, who visited the "Choctaw, Acolapissa, Natchez, (Muskhogean) Tunica, Atakapa (Tunican)" (Fundaburk, n.p.). John White's paintings show people on the coast of Carolina wearing feather capes.

Southeastern women used their homespun cloth to make mantles as well as skirts: "When it is hot, the women wear only a mantle in the shape of a skirt, but when the cold makes itself felt, they wear a second, the middle of which passes under the right arm, the two corners being fastened on the left shoulder. In this manner the two arms are free and only one breast is visible" (Swanton 1911, 53).

The term "matchcoat" is said to come from an Algonquin word, *gwashunk*, which, as recorded in the Narragansett language by John Williams in 1643, seems to be the root word for coat. *Tummockgwashunk* was beaver coat, for example. Europeans would have heard this term from people near the coasts, and perhaps garbled it into matchcoat, a term that made sense to them in English because it included the word "coat." This term for a mantle became common throughout the Southeast as woolen broadcloth replaced indigenous materials. The Cherokee word is *ahnawo utana* or big cloth, literally "cloth it-grew." The word for ribbon was *agwelosdi*, which also refers to the part in one's hair. Perhaps the straightness of the ribbons and trims reminded Cherokees of the parting of the hair.

After the Cherokees began trading for stroud cloth in the early 1700s, this fabric became common in match coats, in red or blue, with various kinds of trim and decoration. Describing the Cherokees in 1756, DeBrahm said:

> *If they have a Blanket or a Piece of Strout [stroud] (by them called a Watch-Coat) to hang about them as a Mantle in the day time, and to roll themselves in it at Night, they are satisfied, as they use very little else to cover their Body or Head, unless their Legs and Feet, which they always keep rapt up in leather Socks (Mockasins) and woollen Leggings. (DeBrahm, 1971, 109)*

The matchcoat was a length of wool broadcloth, usually red or dark blue, from fifty-four to sixty-three inches wide (the width of a piece of cloth) and from sixty-five to seventy-two inches long. (For more detail on stroud cloth, see the chapter on breechclouts, this volume.) In trade agreements and lists of prices, stroud for a matchcoat is usually specified as two yards, or seventy-two inches. In the list of gifts for the Cherokees who came to fight as allies in 1759, General Amherst specifies, for one hundred warriors, on their return: "100 Blue Strowd Cloth Match Coats. 1 yd. 3/4 & 2 inches each" (Mays, 74–77). This would produce a matchcoat of sixty-five inches in length.

Matchcoats were usually decorated. Bartram, describing Cherokees, Choctaws, and Creeks, said, "They have a large mantle of the finest cloth they are able to purchase, always either of scarlet or blue colour; this mantle is fancifully decorated, with rich lace or fringe round the border, and often with little round silver, or brass bells" (1998, 122). Adair's confirms this description for the southeastern Indians: "The young Indian men and women, through a fondness of their ancient dress, wrap a piece of cloth round them . . . about a fathom square [six feet] bordered seven or eight quarters deep, to make a shining cavalier of the beau monde, and to keep out both the heat and cold" (70).

Presents to delegations, payment to warriors, and lists of trade items and their prices included significant amounts of ribbon, tapes, and trims. For example, General Amherst's gifts to the Cherokee warriors included three hundred yards of caddis (wool worsted tape), three yards of green and yellow ribbon for each pair of leggings, for a total of three hundred yards, and for each of twenty

AUSTENACO, Great Warriour,
Commander in Chief of the Cherokee Nation.

"Austenaco, Great Warriour /
Commander in Chief of the Cherokee Nation." *British Magazine* 3
(July 1762): 378. Note match coat
tucked over right shoulder and
draped. Courtesy of the Duane
King collection.

warriors who distinguished themselves, twenty-four yards of bed lace. This is a
sturdy trim of wool, linen, and silk combinations, woven with a figured pattern,
from one and a quarter to three inches wide. On a matchcoat two yards long, this
gift would create eleven or twelve rows of bed lace. (Some of the length of the
lace is taken up as it is applied.)

In the Cherokee trade, in 1751 and in 1762 the price of a matchcoat, or two
yards of stroud, was three buck skins or six doe skins. The price of ribbons,
tapes, and trims varied, with gold lace being the most expensive, followed by
bed lace, silk ribbon, and other trims including caddis, gartering, none-so-pretty,
and so on.

Mantles were included in the expenses for Cherokees traveling to England,
both the cloth and the tailoring. When Edmund Montagu was estimating the
cost of taking three Cherokees to England in 1765, he included not only scarlet
cloth but also the "making of mantles." The clothing and expenses of Ostenaco,
Pigeon, and Woyi were well documented on the 1762 trip with Henry Timberlake. English newspapers reported on their dress and provided illustrations.
When they met with King George III, the *Monthly Chronicle* reported, "Ostenaco dressed for the occasion in a mantle of rich blue covered with lace. . . . The
other two Cherokees wore scarlet richly adorned with gold lace" (Timberlake,
136).

Cherokee Peace Delegation from the Electronic Field Trip (EFT) Emissaries of Peace, produced by Colonial Williamsburg and the Museum of the Cherokee Indian. L to R: Bo Taylor, Sonny Ledford, Bullet Standingdeer (Ostenaco), Eddie Swimmer, and Gregory Hunt. Colonial Williamsburg Foundation.

Red wool cape for a child, leather ties. Made by Nancy and Johnnie Ruth Maney for Dvdaya Swimmer. Courtesy of the Collection of Micah Swimmer and Carrah Shawnee Swimmer.

When the Museum of the Cherokee Indian recreated a life-size figure of Oste-naco for the exhibit "Emissaries of Peace," his mantle of navy blue wool was covered with twelve strips of gold metallic trim, following this description. (See color illustration of this figure.)

When Ostenaco sat for his portrait for Sir Joshua Reynolds, he was wearing a red matchcoat with broad stripes of gold lace. Another matchcoat of navy with a border of gold lace may be draped over the arm of his chair. (See color illustration of Ostenaco.)

Both of these resemble garments in the lithograph made in 1762 of the three Cherokees. When Cunne Shote sat for his portrait by Francis Parsons, however, he was wearing a mantle over one shoulder that bears no resemblance to a Cherokee mantle or matchcoat in any other portrait or description. People have speculated about the origin of this garment. Part of it resembles the collar of a military coat, red faced with navy and decorated with gold trim, while the rest resembles a solid red cape. Whatever its construction, it was atypical for a Chero-kee mantle.

Some Cherokees may also have worn the woolen capes that were fashionable during this period. These were often a circular piece of wool with a hood, and some were red.

How to Make and Wear the Matchcoat

MATERIALS

Heavy wool material of red or blue, coating weight, like a blue blazer for winter but not as heavy as a blanket.

MATERIALS FOR DECORATION

Silk ribbon at least one inch wide, either matte, shiny, grosgrain, or moiré.

Bed lace, which is not the same as modern lace but a woven tape about one and a half inches wide with raised figures in it.

Beadwork, on the silk ribbon or on the edging.

Bells, such as round bells, sleigh bells, hawks bells; cones; cones with deer hair dyed red or white; cones of silver, copper, or brass; thimbles.

CUTTING THE MATCHCOAT

1. Cut a piece of wool cloth, red or blue, folded in half lengthwise, about sixty-five to seventy-two inches long.

For a child, make the length about the height of the child, or a little more so he or she can grow into it.

TRIMMING WITH RIBBON

2. Trim lengthwise with silk china ribbon. The ribbon should be at least one inch, and up to one and a quarter inches, wide. The Cherokees' favorite colors for ribbon were yellow, green, red, and blue.

3. Sew the ribbon to the back of the match coat close to the edge, using about six to ten straight stitches per inch.

4. Turn the matchcoat over and sew the ribbon to the front.

5. Add as many rows of ribbon as desired. The most on any match coat was twelve rows, or twenty-four yards. Ribbon can be spaced an inch or so apart or sewn right next to each other.

BINDING

6. Option 1 for binding: Add ribbon binding along the edge perpendicular to the rows of ribbon. Go to the top of the last row of ribbon and allow several inches to hang down as decoration.

7. Option 2 for binding: Add ribbon binding all around the edge of the matchcoat, turning and sewing as with the lengthwise rows of ribbon.

8. Miter the corners.

TRIMMING WITH HEAVY TRIM

9. Sew bedlace or metal trims flush with the edge of the wool. Do not attempt to bind. Most examples show spaces between the rows. Binding the horizontal edge is optional.

BEADWORK DECORATION

10. Beadwork was added in single rows of geometric shapes, or as edging. The beads were often white and about size 8.

Edging: place one bead lying flat alternating with one standing up. It was also done with two flat, two standing.

Geometric designs: scrolls were common in this period, in lines of single beads, as well as triangles.

            Cherokee patterns from stamped pottery or baskets were likely used.

OTHER DECORATION

Some matchcoats were also trimmed with bells, cones, thimbles, and other items.

WEARING THE MATCHCOAT

Traditionally, men and women wore the matchcoat over the left shoulder. It can be folded in half or in three quarters for a more draped look. Sometimes it was wrapped around the body chest-high and tucked in for convenience. In rain, wind, or cold weather, it could be worn over the head. Matchcoats were also used as blankets for sleeping on the ground.

8 Feather Capes, Mantles, and Blankets

feathers applied to cloth
fastened to netting
incorporated into twine
feathers from swans, turkeys,
*   and flamingoes*
how to make feather capes

Cherokees in 1762 in the Overhill Towns still talked about the feather garments they had made and worn, a tradition that was longstanding among the Cherokees and other southeastern tribes. These were described as mantles, or match coats by European observers. The Cherokee word for feather is *ugidali* and the word for match coat is *ahnawo utana*, but we have no record of what Cherokee people called these garments and blankets. Cherokee women were still making these in 1776, and Cherokee people in 1830 still recalled one of the techniques used.

Feather Capes and Blankets

Three kinds of feather capes were made. One was made by placing overlapping rows of feathers on cloth, in the same way that birds' feathers overlap. Another was made by fastening feathers to a base of netting made of twine from plants. The third and most time-consuming technique added downy feathers into twine, resulting in a feather rope. These were then fastened together to make garments.

Both men and women wore these garments for warmth. There is no indication that they were a sign of status among the Cherokees. People describing the Cherokees said that their clothing did not indicate status. Only actions gave them status. Some descriptions mention women wearing feather capes over one shoulder. They also wore feather dresses, tied over one shoulder and reaching to the knee. Feather blankets also provided warmth.

Evidence

The earliest evidence we have of feather capes in the Southeast comes from shell carvings and gorgets from a thousand years earlier, which show dancers wearing masks of birds and capes with long feathers.

Long turkey feather cape from museum exhibit. Courtesy of the Museum of the Cherokee Indian collection.

Feather cape, eighteenth-century style. Cape created by Deborah Harding. Goose feathers simulate white swan feathers, attached to a netted base of hemp, with ties of hand spun dogbane (*Apocynum cannabinum*). Courtesy of the Barbara R. Duncan collection.

Birdman gorget.

Fragment of feather cape from Spiro Mound. Courtesy of the National Museum of the American Indian collection.

Engraving "On of the Religeous men in the towne of Secota" by G. Veen (printed 1590) based on watercolor "Indian Priest" by John White, from the coast of Virginia. Turkey feather cape. Courtesy of the John Carter Brown Library at Brown University.

In 1527, Cabeza DeVaca, travelling along the Gulf coast of Florida, said that the tribes in the high mountains to the north traded feather capes for shells from the coast (Swanton 1911). Presumably these were the Cherokees. In 1585, John White made drawings of Indians on the coast of Carolina, two of which show men in waist-length turkey feather mantles, fastened on one shoulder, reproduced in Fundaburk's volume (1958, n p).

William Bartram traveled through the Southeast from 1773 to 1776, and in writing about the Creeks and Cherokees said: "The women yet amuse themselves in manufacturing some few things, as Belts & Coronets for their Husbands, feathered cloaks, macasens, &c." (1995, 151). In describing the mantles and match coats they wore, he added, "Some have a short cloak, just large enough to cover the shoulders and breast; this is most ingeniously constructed, of feathers woven or placed in a natural imbricated manner, usually of the scarlet feathers of the flamingo, or others of the gayest color" (1995, 122).

James Adair, who lived with the Chickasaws and Cherokees from 1735 to about 1770, reported:

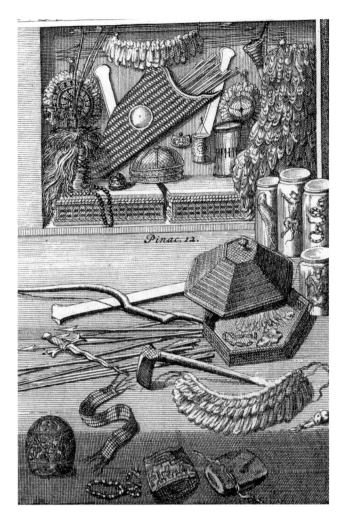

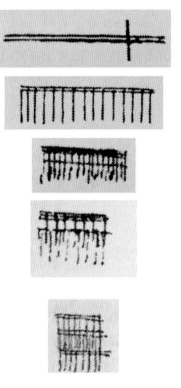

Detail of illustration by Vincent Levinus showing feather capes at top and bottom, collected in North America. From *Wondertooneel der Nature: A Cabinet of Curiosities*, vol. 2, 1715.

Illustration of feather blanket technique from Payne manuscript.

> *They likewise make turkey feather blankets with the long feathers of the neck and breast of that large fowl—they twist the inner end of the feathers very fast into a strong double thread of hemp, or the inner bark of the mulberry tree, of the size and strength of coarse twine, as the fibres are sufficiently fine, and they work it in the manner of fine netting. As the feathers are long and glittering, this sort of blanket is not only very warm, but pleasing to the eye.*
> *(411–12)*

Descriptions of native people making feather mantles in Louisiana in the 1750s appear to match descriptions of Cherokee feather mantles as well, but provide a few more details.

> *With the thread which they obtain from the bark of the bass tree they make for themselves a kind of mantle which they cover with the finest swan feathers fastened on this cloth one by one, a long piece of work in truth, but they account their pains and time as nothing when they want to satisfy themselves. The feather mantles are worked on a frame similar to that on which*

Feather bag from Peru. Handspun and handwoven cloth, feathers attached with additional bands of cloth. Feathers are dyed and trimmed to about 2 inches in length. Anonymous collection.

wig makers work hair. They lay out the feathers in the same manner and fasten them to old fish nets or old mulberry-bark mantles. They place them in the manner already outlined one over another and on both sides. For this purpose they make use of little turkey feathers. The women who can obtain feathers of the swan or Indian duck make mantles of them. (Swanton 1911, 63)

In the 1820s, Rev. Daniel Sabine Buttrick and John Howard Payne were collecting information from the oldest Cherokee people, whose memories encompass the years 1750 to 1820. They described in detail one technique used to make turkey-feather blankets and "cloth for short gowns." (In the eighteenth century, a "short gown" was a jacket worn by women that covered the shoulders, upper arms, and body and extended to just below the waist.)

The feathers, being plucked off, were rubbed, and made as soft as possible. Then a narrow strip of soft, pliable bark, as long as the blanket was to be wide, was put down, and feathers placed on it, from end to end. Then a similar strip of bark was laid on the top, and these two strips of bark were sowed, or fastened together with bark thread. Then another strip was put und[er], and another tier of feathers & strip of bark over & so on, till one or more blankets were finished.

The women also made cloth for short gowns in the same way. This cloth was pleasant to wear and beautiful. The feathers are an inch or inch and a half long. (vol. 2, 179)

Cloth, twine, and feathers all deteriorate rapidly in the acidic ground and in the damp climate of the Southeast, so no complete feather cape artifacts remain for the Cherokees—only a few fragments, preserved by their proximity to copper. Fortunately, descriptions of Cherokee feather capes exist, and we can extrapolate additional details from descriptions from other sources. Some of these are from other southeastern tribes.

The only surviving examples seem to be from the "feather rope" method of incorporating downy feathers into a cord, then weaving a cape with these cords. Feather-cape fragments, from the Spiro Mound, were examined by John Standingdeer Jr. at the National Museum of the American Indian; their feathers were wrapped with a technique similar to that used in tying flies for trout fishing. This may have been what created the "pile" observed by de Soto's chroniclers. Analysis of feather-cape fragments from the Etowah Mounds determined that they were made of small downy feathers from swans, geese, or ducks, dyed red and gold, incorporated into dark brown yarn; the relationship of the yarn to the feathers could not be determined because the materials were too fragile (Sibley, et al.). The technique of adding threads on top of feathers already twined into ropes also is used in Maori and Hawaiian feather capes.

When Deborah Harding began working with the Museum of the Cherokee Indian to construct a feather cape on a base made from knotted netting for the "Emissaries of Peace" exhibit, she consulted examples of featherwork from the Amazon for ideas on how to attach the feathers. Ethnographic accounts say that feathers were individually attached. Some Mayan and Hawaiian featherwork also shows examples of feathers attached to a netted base. An artifact from Peru recently examined by the author had feathers attached to cloth using the exact method described by Cherokee people in the 1820s.

Featherwork in the Eighteenth Century

The Cherokees used feathers in many ways. Feather wands and entire wings were exchanged between nations as signs of peace or war. The Cherokee delegation of 1730 gave an eagle tail to the King of England as a token of their relationship. White wings of swans sent to other nations meant peace, while swans' wings painted red and black meant war (Adair, 284). The person who painted feathers for warriors to wear followed certain rituals. A white swan's wing was used by Beloved Women and signified their position. Indeed, a swan's wing was found with a burial in the Mississippian period (Chapman 1985, 86). Feather wands were used in dances, especially wands made of eagle feathers, also known as "calumets." Feathers were attached to pipes. Players in the stickball game wore feathers that signified their abilities. Men and women wore feathers, wings, and even entire birds as personal adornment.

Feathers available to the Cherokees in the eighteenth century included many birds known today, as well as several extinct birds such as the passenger pigeon and Carolina parakeet. They used feathers from the golden eagle, bald eagle, several kinds of hawks, swan, wild turkey, cardinal, heron, buzzard, raven, golden flicker, several varieties of woodpeckers, and others. There is no evidence of owl feathers being used, perhaps because of the negative associations with some owls. Feathers may have been among items obtained in trade. Bartram comments on feather capes made from flamingo feathers among the Creeks and Cherokees.

Cloth and Twine in the Eighteenth Century

Making twine from plant fibers goes back at least 9,500 years in the southern Appalachians. At this time, people made impressions with twine on their clay hearths, which, after being baked by fire, survived in the archaeological record. The use of twine to make fish nets dates back at least ten thousand years, to the early Archaic period, as evidenced by the large number of net weights found in the archaeological record.

Cherokees were making cloth more than three thousand years ago. We know this because the earliest pottery, Swannanoa pottery from about 1000 BC, found near present-day Swannanoa, North Carolina, had fabric pressed onto the damp clay. Plants commonly used for twine and cloth included mulberry bark, nettles, milkweed species, dogbane (*Apocynum* species) and basswood. Other fibers were spun and woven, and their use continued into the eighteenth century. These included buffalo hair, deer hair, dog hair, rabbit hair, and possum hair. (For more information on Cherokee cloth, see chapter 6, this volume.) For a list of plants and animal fibers used in Cherokee textiles, see appendix F. Feather capes could have been used in very ancient times by the Cherokee, but there is no record of this. We can only speculate that if they made nets for fishing ten thousand years ago, they possibly could have attached feathers to them to make garments. An example of this comes from the Pacific. In Hawaii, capes made of fishnets had ti-leaves attached to them to serve as raincoats centuries before feathers were attached to the same type of fishnet base (Hiroa).

Making Feather Capes Today

Cherokee feather capes have been re-created in the mid-twentieth and early twenty-first centuries by the Eastern Band of Cherokee Indians. Capes made of long wild turkey feathers sewn onto a cloth backing were created for the outdoor drama *Unto These Hills* and were worn by the character of the Cherokee chief who greets Hernando de Soto in 1540. One of these capes is on display in the permanent exhibit at the Museum of the Cherokee Indian. Long tail feathers are sewn onto a burlap backing, and there were several rows of breast feathers around the neck of the garment.

About 2002, some Cherokee women asked me to find out more about feather capes. This research took several years, but by 2005 I had gathered enough information to proceed, and I personally commissioned Deborah Harding at the Carnegie Museum of Natural History to create a feather cape on a twined base for the "Emissaries of Peace" exhibit. Since then, Harding has made additional feather capes, and she has conducted workshops on netting and feather cape making at the Museum of the Cherokee Indian and Cherokee women of the Eastern Band have begun making feather mantles once again, as well as the nets that form their bases. Several have been worn by Cherokee women in the Miss Cherokee pageants. As in the 1500s, they are considered treasures because of the time needed to create them.

Cherokee women in Oklahoma have also begun recreating feather capes. Lisa Rutherford and Shawna Cain have both made feather capes, and Cain received

Best of Show at the Cherokee Art Market in 2011 for her long turkey feather cape. Robert Perry of the Chickasaw Nation has recreated the long, turkey feather capes and written about the process (Perry, 2009).

Note that raptors and songbirds and their feathers are protected by federal law. Feather mantles being recreated at the Museum have used goose feathers obtained from commercial craft suppliers. Goose satinette feathers about three inches long provide a good approximation of other feathers and can be obtained in a variety of colors. About half a pound is needed to make one feather mantle. Wild turkey feathers are available from a variety of sources. Some states have a hunting season on swans, and their feathers can be legally obtained there.

How to Make a Feather Cape

These instructions are for making a feather cape on a base of cloth, one of the original methods. This method is described by Cherokee elders in the Payne manuscript. It also resembles the featherwork of other tribes.

You can also make a feather cape on a netted base, if you have the skill to make the net, or a contact with someone who does. Using commercial netting made for crafts does not work very well because it is not stiff enough. Feathers must be attached to the netted base one by one, a task that would require at least one hundred hours of work.

MATERIALS

Cloth for cape: This should be lightweight enough to drape but heavy enough to hold the feathers. Heavyweight linen, cotton, or hemp fabric will work. Canvas is too heavy. Muslin is too light.

Bias tape to hold feathers in place: This can be cotton/poly bias tape, or cotton twill tape. Cotton twill tape will hold up better. Depending on the size of the feathers, this should be about three-eighths to one-half of an inch wide. It should match the color of the feathers.

Ties for front: About one yard of hemp twine or other natural-fiber cord.

Feathers:

Wild turkey: Wild turkey feathers of several different kinds can be used, depending on the effect you want. The long tail feathers with iridescent tips work well on the longer, knee-length cape. You can then use the smaller breast feathers around the collar.

The wing-tip feathers work well on an elbow-length cape.

The small breast feathers also work well on an elbow-length cape but will require more time to attach.

Goose: Goose "satinette" feathers make a good substitute for the "feathers of brightly colored songbirds." These are commercially available and can be purchased by weight, in different colors. About one-quarter to one-half of a pound is enough for a cape, depending on the size of the person. Because songbirds and their feathers are protected by law, you must substitute red goose feathers for cardinal feathers; bright blue goose feathers for bluebird feathers; green and gold goose feathers for Carolina parakeet feathers; black goose feathers for crow or raven feathers; and white goose feathers for swan feathers. (Swan feathers can be legally obtained in states on the east coast that have a hunting season on swans.)

INSTRUCTIONS

1. Measure the desired length of your cape, from the base of the neck to either the elbow or the knee.

2. For an elbow-length cape, cut a circle of cloth with a radius of that length plus four inches. Cut a slit up the center front, from the edge to the center of the circle. This will be the front of your cape. Hem the cloth on all edges to keep it from raveling.

3. Sort feathers into piles of small, medium, and large.

4. Discard any feathers that are broken or have damaged tips.

5. Sort feathers into right and left small, right and left medium, and right and left large. (It is handy to store them in Ziploc bags, marked with Sharpie.)

6. Make a strip of feathers by sewing together two pieces of twill tape, with the quills of feathers between them. Make sure that your hand or machine stitching pierces the quills to hold them in place. Space the feathers so that they are barely touching at the widest part of the feather.

7. When sewing, make sure that all the feathers are either curved in or out. "Curved in" refers to the way the feathers lie naturally on the bird. "Curved out" means that you flip over the feathers so that the side facing toward the bird's body is now facing out, away from the cloth part of the cape and the body of the wearer.

8. Measure around the bottom of your cape and make the first strip of feathers half that length plus a few inches. Make the bottom strip with the biggest feathers. Make one of the strips with right-hand feathers and the other with left-hand feathers.

9. Sew the strips directly onto the cloth cape. Sew the first row with the tape just above the hem of the cape, so the feathers hang down below it. Sew the tape with right-hand feathers to the right-hand side of the cape and the tape with left-hand feathers to the left-hand side of the cape. Make them meet evenly in the back center.

10. Make your next two strips of feathers slightly shorter in length, to match the size of the cape. Continue to use the large left-hand and right-hand feathers. Place the second row so that the ends of the feathers cover the twill tape from the first row, like shingles on a roof. See the illustration from the Payne manuscript, page 95.

11. Repeat steps eight and nine until you have covered the cloth with rows of feathers. Plan your rows so that you cover the cape with large feathers at the bottom, medium-size feathers in the middle, and the smallest feathers at the top.

12. Finish off the twill tape with the last row of feathers around the neck as follows. Add an additional piece of twill tape, folded over the neckline, to cover the ends of the quills. If you prefer, you can add a row of small feathers sewn by hand to this finishing tape.

13. Where the neckline comes together, insert a piece of twine on each side into the last finishing twill tape. Fasten the twine securely by sewing it by hand. You can add a bead or two on the ends of the twine to make it lie down.

14. To store your feather cape, turn it inside out and roll it lightly together. Groom feathers by hand as needed to restore its shape before wearing. Clean feathers by placing a window screen over the garment. Hold the hose of a vacuum cleaner several inches above the screen and move it back and forth to gently suction dirt from the feathers.

9   *Moccasins and Their Decoration*

‖ ◆‖

Europeans learned the word "moccasin" from American Indians along the Atlantic coasts who spoke related languages. In 1643, Roger Williams documented the word "mocussinass" for shoes among the Narragansett Indians of present-day Rhode Island (Williams). This was similar to the word *makasin* used by tribes in Virginia; *makizin* used by Anishinabe people; and *m'kusun* of the Micmac, all Algonquin languages.

The Cherokee word for shoe is *alasulo* (one shoe) or *dilasulo* (shoes), as documented in 1756 and still used today. But a separate word for moccasins survived into the 1880s: *tsvtsawodi*, a pair of moccasins. These Cherokee shoes, as observed in the eighteenth century, were made of leather and often decorated. Adults and children frequently went barefoot, *nulasvdlv'i*, but wore shoes when traveling away from home, going to war, and on trading expeditions. They were also worn when people dressed up for dances in the townhouse, as Bartram described at the Cherokee town of Cowee in 1776.

As noted in chapter 1, shoes and slippers twined from plant fibers were found in the historical Cherokee area, dating back more than three thousand years. Outside the Cherokee area shoes and sandals made from plant fibers date back 7,500 years on the Missouri River, in caves in the Ozarks, on the Colorado Plateau, and in Oregon (Kuttruff, et al.).

People around the world have used leather and plant fibers to make footwear for millennia. About six thousand years ago, Egyptian pharaohs and upper-class people wore leather sandals, while poorer people made their shoes of reeds. A recent discovery in Armenia has been touted as the world's oldest known leather shoe, at about 5,500 years old. It is made of cowhide, tanned, and laced with leather through eyelets along a gathered center seam. Also in Europe, a man's mummified body found in the Alps and dated to about 5,200 years ago was wearing shoes made with bearskin soles and deerskin panels. Four-thousand-

Moccasins, groundhog skin with thongs of squirrel skin. Collected by James Mooney on Qualla Boundary ca. 1880s. "Moccasins (Dilasula): Each made of a single piece of groundhog skin sewed with thongs of squirrel skin, all tanned in Indian fashion and afterward well greased." Courtesy of the Smithsonian National Museum of Natural History collection.

year-old leather shoes in northern China were made from sheep hide. Nomadic indigenous people in that area also used yak hide, deer skin, fish skins, and wool for footgear. About three thousand years ago, Olmec people in Central America developed technology that combined latex from tree species with the sap of morning glories to create rubber soled shoes, molded to the individual's foot.

While most of the American Indian tribes had a similar form of leather footwear during the eighteenth century, differences in style and decoration distinguished northeastern tribes, southeastern tribes, and individual tribes. Most of the southeastern tribes wore center-seam or pucker-toe moccasins, which as the name suggests had a center seam gathered vertically from the toes toward the ankle. Cherokee moccasins resembled Creek moccasins in that the center seam began near the ends of the toes, but Cherokee moccasins were distinctive in that two small cuts made a tab centered on the heel that was folded up and sewn in place.

Southeastern moccasins were first described in print in 1705 in Robert Beverly's "The History and Present State of Virginia . . . By a Native and Inhabitant of the Place," which was published in London: "Their shoes, when they wear any, are made of an entire piece of Buck-Skin; except when they sow a piece to the bottom, to thicken the soal [*sic*]. They are fasten'd on with running Strings, the Skin being drawn together like a Purse on the top of the Foot, and tyed round the Ankle. The Indian name of this kind of Shoe is Mocasin" (Swanton 1946, 464).

Cherokee and Creek shoes are described by William Bartram in 1793 as being made by women (1995, 127). Bartram continues, "The moccasin defends and adorns the feet; they seem to be an imitation of the ancient buskin or sandal; these are very ingeniously made of deer skins, dressed very soft, and curiously ornamented according to fancy" (1995, 122).

Moccasins were made from various animal hides, but the most popular was buckskin from the white-tailed deer. The technological accomplishment of brain-tanning and smoking was quite marvelous to Europeans in the eighteenth century, as their comments show, regarding the deerskin trade. Brain-tanning and smoking renders leather soft, pliable, and water-resistant. If it becomes wet, it can be easily dried and retains its size and shape. This quality makes brain-

(*above, left*) Moccasins from NMNH, detail of center seam with additional stitching in every pucker. Courtesy of the Smithsonian National Museum of Natural History collection.

(*above*) Moccasins from NMNH, detail of heel construction with added piece of leather decoration. Courtesy of the Smithsonian National Museum of Natural History collection.

(*left*) Moccasins made by Richard Saunooke, Eastern Band of Cherokee Indians, early twenty-first century. Note details of stitching and triangular piece, characteristic of Cherokee moccasins. Courtesy of the Bradley Welch collection.

tanned footwear quite comfortable and much appreciated by the wearer, especially in the damp climate of the southern Appalachians. The possible fragility of the buckskin is mitigated by the addition of a heavier sole, sewn to the outside of the moccasin. Cherokee men traveling on war expeditions carried several pairs of moccasins with them, and also supplies to mend them. When Timberlake traveled with a large party of Cherokees from Chota to Williamsburg, they stopped at Fort Robinson, and he noted matter-of-factly: "We remained here all next day to rest ourselves and mend our mockasons, tho' such fine weather was scarce to be lost . . ." (Timberlake, 53).

Tribes throughout North America used animal brains to tan hides. It is a laborious process that begins with soaking and scraping the deerskin so that the inside and outside are smooth. One observer noted that deer's brains were made into a cake (a solid mass) and then baked in the fire before being soaked in water and applied to the skins (Swanton 1946, 444). Others said that the brains were used fresh. A saying still circulates in the oral tradition: each animal has just enough brains to tan its own hide. The brains remain on the skin or soak with the skin for a time. Then the skins are rinsed, dried, stretched, and scraped. They must be worked by hand to become pliable. Finally they are smoked, an important part of the process because it makes them water-resistant.

The naturalist Mark Catesby described the smoking process in the early eighteenth century as involving "digging a hole in the earth, arching it over with hoop-sticks, over which the skin is laid . . . under that is kindled a slow fire, which is continued until it is smoked enough" (Swanton 1946, 444).

In addition to being tanned, hides were dyed. Native plants and dyeing techniques were used to create colors for Cherokee baskets and cloth. The hulls, bark, and root bark of walnut and butternut yield a black dye, which was used on some moccasins. Cherokee elders in 1830 said that in the old days, war chiefs wore special red-dyed moccasins. This red dye could have come from bloodroot, which is used as a basket dye, or from red ochre mixed with oil and rubbed into the leather. White moccasins are also described in the 1700s, and they may have been processed somehow with white clay, kaolin, which is found in the Cherokee country.

According to Cherokee elders' descriptions of ceremonies, the wives of the priests wore white moccasins: "Their moccasins were white also, and made like eastern boots, coming up about halfway to the knee" (Payne, vol. 2, 20).

While moccasins worn everyday were plain, those used for special occasions were greatly decorated in the 1700s, with natural materials such as spurs from the wild turkey and the hooves of baby deer, which produced a musical rattling sound. Materials obtained in trade were also used. In 1775, Adair commented, "The young warriors now frequently fasten bell-buttons, or pieces of tinkling brass to their maccaseenes, and to the outside of their boots, instead of the old turkey-cock-spurs which they formerly used" (202).

The same items used to adorn leggings apparently were used on moccasins, including bells. In addition, silk ribbons were not only sewn on moccasins but also tied ornamentally around them. Engravings of Cherokees visiting London in 1762 show silk ribbons tied around their moccasins, with a prominent bow at the front.

A pair of moccasins in the collections of Colonial Williamsburg, dated to 1750, are decorated with two colors of silk moire ribbon, white glass beads applied in geometric patterns on the ribbon and used for edging, tin cones with red yarn, and strips of decorated ribbon or gartering covering the seams at the heel and toe. In addition, individual white beads are sewn into each pucker of the center seam. While these are more likely from the Great Lakes area and not specifically Cherokee, they do show some of the forms of decoration of the time.

Henry Timberlake described another form of moccasin decoration, one that has created some controversy. He says that Cherokee moccasins were "ornamented with porcupine quills." He also describes quillwork on a Cherokee ceremonial pipe. The only other description of Cherokee quillwork comes from William Bartram, who says that a diadem or band around the head may be decorated with "stones, beads, wampum, porcupine quills, &c." (1995, 121). Bartram is speaking of both the Cherokees and Creeks.

Moccasins, America, 1750–1780, deerskin leather, silk ribbon, metallic braid, glass beads, tin cones, wool yarn, linen thread, acc# 1999-73, 1-2. Although these moccasins are not Cherokee, they do show the characteristic decorations of the 1700s. Courtesy of the Colonial Williamsburg Foundation.

Generally quillwork is associated with Great Lakes or Great Plains tribes. They produced bags, garters, leggings, pipes, and many other beautiful items decorated with quillwork in the eighteenth century. Quillwork was also common, however, among the Cherokees and other southeastern tribes in the eighteenth century. For example, in the early 1700s, the Natchez people along the Mississippi River (present-day Louisiana) understood how to process, dye, and sew decoratively with these quills. Details of these processes, using large quantities of quills, are described by Le Page Du Pratz. Natchez women even wore porcupine quills in their hair (Swanton 1911).

While Timberlake describes porcupine quillwork on Cherokee moccasins and on Cherokee pipes, he does not list porcupines among southeastern animals. Outside of ethnographic descriptions, no hard evidence can be found for porcupines living in the southern Appalachians in the eighteenth century. Scholars and archaeologists say that the last documentation of porcupines in the southern Appalachians was about one thousand years ago. Their present range begins around Maryland and continues northward.

The presence of porcupine quills on Cherokee moccasins and pipes could be explained by trade. Cherokees could have traded with tribes to the north for these quills, just as they traded for shells to the south. This trade has not yet been documented, however. Perhaps porcupines remained in some areas of the mountains before becoming extirpated here. Cherokee quillwork remains something of a mystery.

How to Make Cherokee Moccasins

MATERIALS

Leather: Brain-tanned leather is the most expensive but also the most historically accurate material. It is the most comfortable and durable, being water-resistant. You can obtain this leather from sources online. Chrome-tanned leather approximates the quality of brain-tanned leather and is less expensive. Regular, commercially tanned deerskin also works well. You may need two deer hides depending on the size of your foot. You will have scraps left over for other projects.

Sewing material: Artificial sinew or strips of leather cut from the hide at a uniform width, about a quarter inch.

Tools: Sharp knife, sharp scissors, awl, strong needle.

Decorations: Turkey spurs, deer hooves, brass bells, cones, breast buckles, white glass beads, tin cones with yarn, tin cones with deer hair, quillwork.

INSTRUCTIONS

1. Cherokee moccasins were traditionally cut from one piece of leather (for each moccasin). Use heavy paper (from a brown paper grocery bag or craft paper) to make your pattern.

2. Trace your foot.

3. Draw around your foot in the illustrated shape. Allow about a half inch at the heel and toe for sewing. Make sure the curves allow enough room for the leather to cover your instep. When measuring, make the fit just right.

4. Fold your pattern in half to make it symmetrical.

5. Cut your pattern out of leather.

6. You will use three different stitches to make your pucker-toe moccasin. The first is the baseball stitch, which you will begin at the point of the toe, making a knot to hold it in place. Stitch up to within a few inches of the opening for the ankle.

7. When you have finished stitching, pull gently to make the seam pucker. This makes the moccasin fit your foot.

8. Use the second kind of stitch, the running stitch, to secure the seam to within about an inch of the ankle opening.

9. Use the third kind of stitch, the whip stitch or overhand stitch, to sew up the seam at the back of the moccasin.

10. If you want to add another protective sole, stand again with your foot on paper, this time wearing your moccasins. Trace around your right foot and your left foot. They may be different. Use this tracing to cut a piece of leather—it can be the same as your moccasin leather or a heavier type such as elk or groundhog.

11. Sew the protective sole directly to the outer sole of your moccasin with simple running stitches. You will have to use an awl to pierce the heavier leather. Strips of leather from the heavy leather will make the most durable sewing material.

12. Decorate your moccasins as you prefer. Simple eighteenth-century style included a silk ribbon on the flap, edged with white beads in the edging stitch. Add bells and other items.

CARING FOR YOUR BRAIN-TANNED MOCCASINS

After you wear your moccasins, let them air out. Don't put them away damp. If they get soaked, dry them gently.

WEARING YOUR MOCCASINS

Today, some people like to insert an insole with cushioning between their foot and the bottom of the moccasin, for comfort.

10 *Belts, Garters, Straps, and Pouches*

fingerweaving with beads
twined weaving
weaving with beads

The woven belts, garters, straps, hairpieces, and bags created by Cherokee women formed an important part of the wardrobe of Cherokee men and women and are represented in art works, written descriptions, and a few rare pieces in museum collections. From these we can infer a world of expertise in designing, weaving, dyeing, and decorating, using natural materials and those obtained through trade. These artifacts speak of a world of choices made by Cherokee women artists who were building on traditional designs and experimenting with new materials to express their ideas of what was necessary, beautiful, and Cherokee.

Both Bartram and Adair confirm that the women were the weavers:

The women are the chief, if not the only manufacturers. (Adair, 411)

The women are more vigilant, and turn their attention to various manual employments; they make all their pottery or earthenware, moccasins; spin and weave the curious belts and diadems for the men; fabricate lace, fringe, embroider and decorate their apparel &c, &c. (Bartram 1995, 127)

The Cherokee word for weaving is *gvega*, or "he or she is weaving." Another word, *asdeyoha*, means "he or she is braiding or making rope." Beads in general were called *adela*, and wampum in particular was referred to as *unelsgwaledo* (DeBrahm 1756). Adair describes southeastern women weaving "broad garters, sashes, shot-pouches, broad belts, and the like, which are decorated all over with beautiful strips [stripes] and chequers" (Adair, 411).

To discuss these items of clothing and accessories used by the Cherokees in the 1700s, I want first to list the techniques and materials used, because sometimes the same techniques created different items. Diagonal interlacing, for example, also called oblique fingerweaving, was used to create belts, garters, and hair ornaments. Attention to these items can also provide information about

Fingerwoven sashes made by Karen George on display at Cherokee Voices Festival, Museum of the Cherokee Indian 2012. Photo by Barbara R. Duncan.

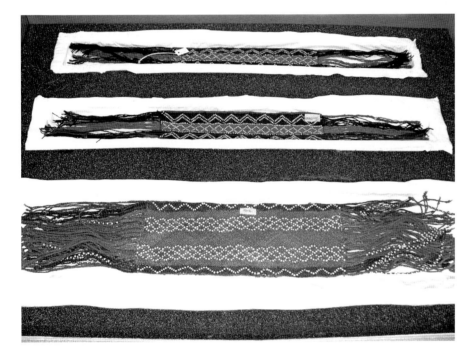

Fingerwoven garters, 1700s. Wool, glass beads. Tribe unknown. American Museum of Natural History, New York. Photo by Deborah Harding.

what designs were considered distinctly Cherokee in the 1700s. Finally, I will describe the specific items that we can document among the Cherokees during this period.

At least four distinct weaving techniques were used during this period: twined weft weaving, twined warp weaving, and diagonal interlacing (also called oblique fingerweaving) used both beads and yarn. In addition, a weaving technique was used to create garters, wampum collars, and wampum belts in long rectangular shapes. Techniques to create netting continued to be used throughout the 1700s to make fishnets, round bags for carrying objects, and the bases of feather capes.

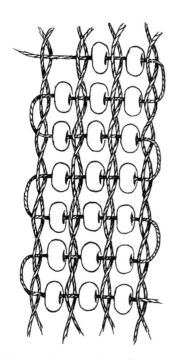

Schematic drawing of twined-warp weaving from Sauk garter. Used in the past by Cherokees and other tribes east of the Mississippi. Drawing by William Orchard (1929, 95).

Sash made of wool and black and white glass beads using twined warp weaving. Attached to powder horn, probably Cherokee. Other Cherokee examples exist as well with beaded straps. Courtesy of the John and Marva Warnock collection.

Twined weft weaving was used to create cloth and to create bags, as described in earlier chapters. Cloth was created in one large flat piece, while bags were often woven as three-dimensional containers. This three-dimensionality was accomplished by beginning at the bottom of the bag and then weaving continuously around the bag, somewhat in the way that socks are knitted today with circular needles. Bags had a slightly more openwork appearance, achieved by the spacing of weft rows farther apart, and were made of heavier yarns than cloth. Warp (vertical) threads were fastened to a frame the size of the piece, while the maker twined the weft (horizontal) threads and managed the tension. (See descriptions and illustrations of skirts and bags in chapter 1.)

Twined warp weaving in the 1700s was used to create items made entirely of glass beads, usually black and white. This was made possible by the abundance of glass beads available through trade. Woolen worsted yarn formed the warp, usually black, but occasionally red. One piece in a museum appears to be made from brown buffalo hair dyed red. Beads were strung on a continuous weft, with every bead held in place by a twist of two warp threads. Often, black beads formed the background and white beads created the design. Tension was created by fastening the warp threads to an immovable object, while the maker manipulated the weft threads and beads with her hands, keeping appropriate tension while working. This technique was used to create straps, bags, and garters. Some straps made in this way were used to carry powder horns and pouches; others were worn with gorgets or just as ornaments. The strap worn by Ostenaco in the Reynolds painting may have been made this way. Bags

Student in workshop at Museum of
the Cherokee Indian maintains tension
while creating a fingerwoven belt of red
worsted wool and white glass beads.
Photo by Barbara R. Duncan.

and garters depicted in paintings and surviving as artifacts also appear to have
been made in this fashion. All of the above show specifically Cherokee designs
in their patterns of black and white beads. (See color illustration of Ostenaco
painted by Reynolds.)

Diagonal interlacing is also called oblique fingerweaving. It is the same technique as twined weaving, except that the warp and woof are diagonal in relation
to the finished edge of the piece. This requires the weaver to keep careful track
of pairs of threads in the process, and experts handle dozens of pairs to create
wide belts. One end of the piece is fastened to an immovable object, and the
maker uses her hands to maintain the order of the interlacing pairs and keep
the tension on all threads consistent. While doing this, she crosses the threads
in a prescribed order, places beads in specific patterns, and maintains tension to
produce a smooth, symmetrical fabric with geometrical patterns of beads and
colors woven in. Beginning in the 1700s, white glass beads were threaded onto
strands of yarn and placed to form geometrical patterns. In earlier times, shell
beads were used in this way.

Some scholars believe that this technique originated in Europe and that
French traders taught American Indians in Canada how to make the Assomption (or Achigan) sashes for the French voyageurs, but this has been disproven
by Marius Barbeau. He says conclusively that this tradition did not exist in Europe but is widespread in North and South America (Barbeau 1937, 25). In the
southeast, examples of oblique interlacing are found in the Mississippian period,

Cherokee delegation examines wampum belt in historical drama at Colonial Williamsburg, 2010. Belt is made of real wampum in traditional Cherokee design. L to R: Cherokee delegation portrayed by Bo Taylor, Ernest Grant, and Antonio Grant. Governor Dinwiddie portrayed by Dennis Watson. Photo by Barbara R. Duncan.

before contact. (See the illustration of oblique interlacing from Spiro Mound in the introduction.)

The "loom" technique was used to create some belts and garters, in particular wampum belts, wampum collars, and solid beaded garters. The technique does not actually require a loom but refers to the method of weaving. Warp and weft (or woof) threads are vertical and horizontal, respectively; they are separate; and they intersect at right angles.

The production of wampum belts was very important because they were used to send messages of war and peace to indigenous and European nations; they were also used to embody sacred knowledge and stories that were represented in their designs. These belts were kept by the clans. Strings of wampum were given during the reading of treaties and agreements by emissaries, as part of the ceremonies of peace; these also included speech making, dancing, and smoking the pipe. In addition, wampum collars (a broad woven band) were worn by some. "They that can afford it wear a collar of wampum" (Timberlake, 25). The creation of garters woven of beads is not well documented because few examples survive. One rare example was said to have been given by Attakullakulla to Reverend Martin in 1758. Its beads are very small, as are its threads.

New materials were introduced in the 1700s, but Cherokee women continued to use traditional fibers made from plants and from animal hair. They obtained new wool thread by unraveling wool cloth obtained through trade, and they still

Detail of beaded garter, 1758. Blue and white glass beads, threads of plant fibers. Given by Attakullakulla to Rev. Martin in the Overhill Towns. Courtesy of the East Tennessee Historical Society collection.

Garter fingerwoven from buffalo hair with glass beads by Karen George. Buffalo hair and yarn. Courtesy of the Cherokee Historical Association collection.

spun and used plant fibers. Thread made from milkweed fibers has been documented in wampum belts. Thread was spun from the hair of the buffalo, *yansa*; from the black bear, *yona*; and from the white undercoat of the possum, *utsetsdi* (Payne, vol. 2, 50).

Adair said of southeastern women,

> *In the winter season, the women gather buffalo's hair, a sort of coarse brown curled wool; and having spun it as fine as they can, and properly doubled it, they put small beads of different colors upon the yarn, as they work it: the figures they work in those small webs, are generally uniform, but sometimes they diversify them on both sides. (411)*

Dyeing technology was used not only for fibers but also for rivercane splints used in making baskets and mats and for leather. To create red dye, Cherokee women used the rhizomes of bloodroot (*Sanguinaria canadensis*), or *giliwatali* in Cherokee language. Yellowroot (*Xanthorhiza simplicissima*), or *dalonige*, created a yellow color. The black walnut tree (*Juglans nigra*), or *sedi*, provided black walnut hulls, bark, and root bark for black dye. These were combined with butternut (*Juglans cineria*) or *kohi* in Cherokee language, and with sourwood (*Oxydendrum arboreum*) or *nvdogweya* in some recipes.

Cherokee elders described the spinning, weaving, and dyeing traditions of earlier generations who lived in the 1700s:

> *They made many ornamental articles of white hair dyed red, yellow, black &c. They took the white hair of the Opossum, spun it into threads, dyed them,*

some yellow, some black & some a most florid red. These they interwove fancifully to make girdles and garters for the young men, and with the red threads alone they wove or knit the cap of the Itagvsta. Sometimes they spun bears hair for black thread & black cloth. The hair threads were colored yellow by means of a certain root called Ta-lo-ny and black oak bark. Such as was to be colored red, was then put into a dye of blood root. Black was dyed with black walnut, butternut & sourwood. (Payne, vol. 2, 50)

Beads incorporated in weaving originally were made of shell traded from the coasts and processed in Cherokee towns. When glass beads became readily available through the deerskin trade, they were used instead. These were predominantly black and white round beads. In today's bead sizes they would range from size 6 to size 12. Beads made from wampum were either white or purple, depending on which part of the quahog clamshell they were taken from. The shells had larger surfaces of white than purple, so more white beads were created. White and black cylindrical glass beads were manufactured and used in the 1700s to imitate wampum beads as well.

Certain motifs, such as geometric shapes, concentric lines, spirals, and circles, appear in traditional art throughout the world. Some of these motifs are common to American Indian tribes as well. During the Mississippian period, some motifs were popular throughout the Southeast, and it is not always possible to match designs to a specific tribe. When we can identify Cherokee designs, we see them replicated in different media throughout Cherokee culture. For example, the looped path appears in both shell gorgets and incised pottery designs.

We are fortunate to be able to identify some specific designs used in Cherokee culture in the 1700s. Pottery designs found within the Cherokee area during this period have survived, as well as designs on baskets such as those in the British Museum. A few items of clothing, though more perishable, bring to light additional Cherokee designs. These include:

- Interlocking crosses in beaded garter. See illustration on page 113. These are reminiscent of the cross with arms of equal length in the center of the gorget representing the spider bringing the fire.
- Rectangular design in powderhorn strap made of black and white beads joined in twined warp weaving. See illustration on page 110. This design also appears in fingerweaving (oblique interlacing) from the southeast, possibly Cherokee, eighteenth century, in the Marischal Museum in Aberdeen, Scotland.
- Diamond design of white beads on black background interspersed with parallel rows in sash worn by Ostenaco in the Reynolds portrait. This may be made of beads held together with warp twined weaving. See color illustration.
- A design of interlocking long rectangles in a fingerwoven powderhorn sash in a European collection. This was reproduced by Robert Scott Stephenson for the Emissaries of Peace exhibit. See illustration on page 116.

Wampum display by Richard Saunooke at Cherokee Voices Festival, 2013. L to R: wampum belt of reproduction wampum, wampum belt of wampum made of shell, quahog clam shells and conch shell, wampum belt on bow loom at back. Photo by Barbara R. Duncan.

To some extent, the technique of creating these items dictates how designs will take shape. Fingerweaving with beads lends itself to patterns of diamonds and chevrons because an individual strand of yarn moves from side to side obliquely across the finished piece. Designs in wampum belts made with cylindrical beads will always be geometrical in form.

Let's look now at which of these items were in common use in the 1700s. We can state with certainty that Cherokee people created and wore the following items of woven clothing and accessories: belts, garters, hats, hair ornaments, bags, straps, and wampum collars. Artworks from the 1700s, written descriptions, archaeological evidence, rare artifacts, and oral tradition confirm all of these.

Belts or sashes, *adatsosdi*, were woven with diagonal interlacing, and incorporated beads in their designs. Wool from buffalo hair and trade cloth was used. Red and blue trade cloth was unraveled. In addition, functional leather belts were worn. There is evidence that Cherokee women wove belts for men to wear. There is no evidence that women also wore them; on the other hand, there is no evidence that they did not. A few artworks from the time period depict American Indian women in the northeast and Great Lakes region wearing woven belts.

Garters, *dinitsosdi*, were woven in the same manner and were sometimes also decorated with bells (Payne, vol. 2, 50). Both men and women wore garters tied

Fingerwoven sash, wool with glass beads. Created by Robert Scott Stephenson for Emissaries of Peace exhibit. Courtesy of the Museum of the Cherokee Indian collection.

around the upper calf, just below the knee, with or without leggings. The painting on Oconostota's commission shows a man wearing garters without leggings, and a painting created after a 1797 drawing of Toqua shows Cherokee women wearing garters without leggings. Small pieces of fingerweaving with beads, about the size of garters, also appear as hair ornaments and attachments to a southeastern hat in a museum in Scotland.

Garters woven of buffalo hair had particular significance for southeastern women, according to James Adair, who wrote in 1775, "The Indian females continually wear a beaded string round their legs, made of buffalo-hair, which is a species of coarse wool; and they reckon it a great ornament, as well as a preservative against miscarriages, hard labor, and other evils" (201). A fingerwoven garter with white beads believed to be Cherokee is made of buffalo hair dyed red. It is in the collection of the Marischal Museum in Aberdeen, Scotland.

A rare Cherokee beaded garter from 1758, made of tiny white and blue beads, still exists, in the collection of the East Tennessee Historical Society in Knoxville. This garter was given by Attakullakulla to Rev. Martin in 1758 in the Cherokee Overhill town of Chota. It is woven in a loomed style, with glass beads smaller than a size 18 today, on extremely fine thread. Its design features interlocking crosses with arms of equal width.

Garters made of leather may also have been decorated with porcupine quills. Cherokees used porcupine quills to decorate moccasins, leggings, leather capes, and pipe stems in the 1700s.

Straps for Cherokee powder horns and shot pouches in several artifacts and artworks from the 1700s are made using oblique fingerweaving with beads and also using twined warp weaving, or possibly loom weaving with beads. They have a black background with geometric designs in white beads. In addition, a

Note fingerwoven strap with beads. Will Tushka, Cherokee Fall Fair, 2014, waiting to dance with the Warriors of Ani-Kituhwa. Photo by Barbara R. Duncan.

sash worn by Ostenaco in 1762 in London may have been made with this technique. (See color illustration of Ostenaco's portrait by Reynolds.)

These sashes were sometimes attached to bags, which may have been made of leather, wool stroud, or twined fabric. At this time Choctaw people, for example, wove their shot pouches. Men used these bags to carry the black powder, lead shot, and other necessary items for shooting black-powder muskets and rifles. The men also used the bags to carry medicinal herbs such as snakeroot, along with a small bag of parched corn. One member of a war party carried the sacred fire in a small pottery vessel of distinctive shape called a fire pot and was designated the fire carrier, *atsila hyegi*; but most other Cherokee men used some form of leather or cloth bag while traveling.

The functional bags women used to carry items during this period are not as well documented. In their towns and in their houses, they used rivercane baskets and clay pots to store and carry a wide variety of items. They tied baskets on their backs to gather corn in the field. They tied babies to their backs with a

Garters for leggings. Leather with dyed porcupine quills, silk ribbon, and glass beads. Reproduction 11 ⅞" long x 1 ¼" wide. Overall length with ties 45". Anonymous collection.

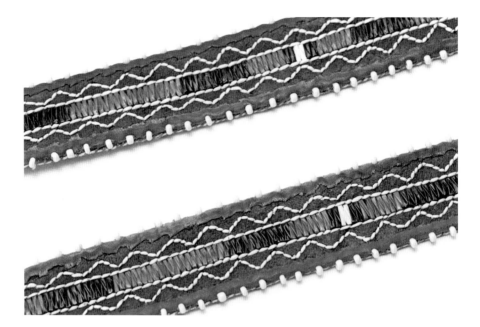

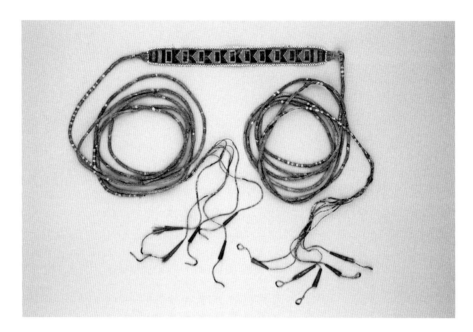

Native American prisoner halter, South Lake Erie Region, 1775–1800, apocynum fiber, quills, sinew, deer or moose hair tufts, metal tinkle cones (hand rolled), glass beads, copper alloy, leather (moosehide?). Acc# 1996-816. Cherokee prisoner ties would have been similar in function but decorated in the southeastern manner with quills, cones, glass beads, deer hair. Courtesy of the Colonial Williamsburg Foundation. Museum Purchase.

length of cloth. If they continued to use the traditional older items during this time, they would have used netted bags to carry large items and twined weft bags to carry smaller items. These twined weft bags originally ranged in size from small (3" x 4") to large (9" x 12") and incorporated dyed stripes. These bags of the 1700s evolved into the elaborate bandolier bags after 1820, beaded in solid panels of colored beads in designs of scrolls, flowers, and other figures.

One more item must be mentioned in this chapter, although evidence is scant. Prisoner ties were twined, woven, braided, and decorated by many tribes throughout the 1700s. These were used to tie prisoners who were brought home from war. They were both functional and decorated. They usually included a band that fastened around the neck, woven in some fashion, and ties that might be as much as twenty feet long, which could be used to tie up a prisoner at night, or to keep them tethered while walking. One example at Colonial Williamsburg, from northeastern tribes, is woven, twined, braided, and embroidered with moose hair. This item must have been important for Cherokees as well, because in order to become a warrior, a man had to capture a prisoner. Then he could advance to the rank of Slave Catcher, and other ranks according to his deeds. If prisoners were adopted into a clan, they became Cherokee, replacing family members who had been killed in war.

How to Make a Bag of Trade Cloth in the Eighteenth-Century Style

MATERIALS

Navy or red heavy wool cloth, about half a yard

(Optional lining of striped linen pillow ticking, red or blue)

White beads, about size 8

Two silver breast buckles (ring brooches)

Decorations: Tin cones with dyed deer hair, bells, etc.

INSTRUCTIONS

1. Cut a rectangle about ten inches wide and twenty inches long.

2. If you want to decorate the bag with beads, sew them on in single rows, creating geometric designs. Avoid beading on a half-inch seam allowance on the lengthwide edges.

3. Fold in half and sew edges to make a bag. Turn right-side out.

4. Cut a strap of the wool cloth about two to three inches wide and at least thirty-six inches long.

5. If you want to decorate the strap, edge with white beads.

6. Fasten the strap to the bag with breast buckles at the side seams.

7. To decorate further, attach tin cones (with or without dyed deer hair) along the folded bottom of the bag so that they hang down.

11 Adornments

body paint

tattooing

hairstyles

jewelry

gorgets

wampum

trade beads

silver

The Cherokees are of a middle stature, of an olive colour, tho' generally painted, and their skins stained with gun-powder, pricked into it in very pretty figures. The hair of their head is shaved, tho' many of the old people have it plucked out by the roots, except a patch on the hinder part of the head, about twice the bigness of a crown-piece, which is ornamented with beads, feathers, wampum, stained deer hair, and such like baubles. The ears are slit and stretched to an enormous size, putting the person who undergoes the operation to incredible pain, being unable to lie on either side for near forty days. To remedy this, they generally slit but one at a time; so soon as the patient can bear it, they are wound round with wire to expand them, and are adorned with silver pendants and rings, which they likewise wear at the nose. This custom does not belong originally to the Cherokees, but take by them from the Shawnese, or other northern nations.

They that can afford it wear a collar of wampum, which are beads cutout of clam shells, a silver breast-plate, and bracelets on their arms and wrists of the same metal.

—Henry Timberlake, Chota, 1762

This chapter will address the various adornments Cherokees wore on their bodies. This includes paint and tattooing; diadems, hairstyles, and ornaments for both men and women; and the profusion of jewelry worn in this period. Cherokees began the century wearing much of their own traditional jewelry made of shell beads, native stones, native pearls, copper, and more. Their role as military partners and trading allies of Britain, France, Spain, Virginia, and South Carolina brought new goods and new styles to them throughout the 1700s. Cherokee warriors had a significant impact on the Yamasee War of 1715 as well as the French and Indian War, and these alliances brought them gifts of silver gorgets, silver armbands, and peace medals. The deerskin trade made new items available to Cherokee people. At first the silver items were manufactured in Europe, but by 1750 colonial silversmiths were making them, and by 1770 Cherokee silversmiths were also creating gorgets, armbands, pierced open-work earrings, and more. In previous generations, Cherokees worked copper into smooth thin sheets and created neckpieces, armbands, and rolled copper beads. In the 1700s, they used silver coins, hammered out, to create earrings, gorgets, and other pieces incised with their own designs of fish, birds, and animals.

Paint and Tattooing

Paint, which was discussed in chapter 2 as part of the general appearance of Cherokee men and women in the 1700s, was called *wodi* or *wohodi*. A tattoo was referred to with the same word for mark and writing, *udoweli*, meaning "it is marked." Observers in the 1700s noted the individual painted styles. Timberlake writes, of his greeting as an emissary of peace about New Year's Day, 1762, in the Overhill Towns:

> *About 100 yards from the town-house we were received by a body of between three and four hundred Indians, ten or twelve of which were entirely naked, except a piece of cloth about their middle, and painted all over in a hideous manner. . . . Cheulah, the headman of the town, led the procession, painted blood red, except his face, which was half-black. (2007, 19)*

Following his stay in the Overhills, Timberlake took three Cherokees on a diplomatic mission to London, initiated by Ostenaco. The great war leader, or Skiagvsta, was accompanied by Woyi (Pigeon) and GvnaShotte (Stalking Turkey). They had a long sea voyage, during which they were on the watch for French ships, for although the Cherokee-Anglo War had ended, the British and French were still at war on land and sea. Upon their safe arrival at Plymouth, Ostenaco painted his face and sang a song of thanks. Timberlake writes, "While in the boat that took us to shore, Ostenaco, painted in a very frightful manner, sung a solemn dirge with a very loud voice to return God thanks for his safe arrival" (2007, 58).

In London their tattoos and paint occasioned many remarks, including written descriptions. Timberlake commented that they wore "a great deal" of vermilion. This detailed description comes from the August 8, 1762, entry in the diary of the Duchess of Northumberland:

> *The Chief [Ostenaco] had the Tail of a Comet revers'd painted on his forehead, his Left Cheek black & His Left Eyelid Scarlet his Rt Eyelid Black and his Right Cheek Scarlet. . . .*
>
> *The second had nothing particular except his eyelids were painted scarlet, the 3rd had painted in Blue on his cheeks a large pair of wings which had*

"Ouatacite, King of the Cherokees."
Court Magazine 1 no. 11 (August 1762):
491. Note tattoos on face and neck,
adornments in hair, gorget and crosses.
Sash around neck could be wampum or
twined-warp weaving with beads. Piece
of hair pulled forward is the same style
as Stalking Turkey in Parsons' portrait.
Courtesy of the Duane King collection.

an odd Effect as he look'd directly as if his Nose & Eyes were flying away.
(Timberlake 2007, 136–37).

From these descriptions, it is clear that some people could not distinguish between the Cherokees' paint and tattoos. Some of the engravings show tattoos on the faces of the Cherokees. Ostenaco seemed to have four parallel horizontal lines tattooed on his forehead, along with an X across each cheek in several engravings. One of the other Cherokees appeared to have intersecting lines in the manner of diamonds on his head. The portrait of GvnaShotte shows a tattoo on his throat of an oval with horizontal lines extending from it wrapping around his neck. A similar tattoo appears on a portrait of a Choctaw chief in London. That and other evidence points to a "language" of tattoos that tribes understood, wherein tattoos indicated war ranks and exploits.

Hairstyles and Ornaments

The hairstyles and ornaments of Cherokee women differed from those of Cherokee men. According to Timberlake, "The women wear the hair of their head, which is so long that it generally reaches to the middle of their legs, and sometimes to the ground, club'd, and ornamented with ribbons of various colours" (2007, 26). They used the berries of red sumac to make a tea that they used as a hair rinse, to keep their hair shiny.

When Timberlake says their hair was "club'd" he means pulled back in a ponytail (in present-day usage) and perhaps doubled over into a bun. Cherokee women used a piece of rivercane split lengthwise and secured with leather tied around it to hold their hair. They may also have ornamented their hair with pieces of fingerweaving, feathers, and silver.

Cherokee men plucked out nearly all the hair of their head, using clam shells, and later metal springs obtained in trade. According to Timberlake, "The hair of their head is shaved, tho' many of the old people have it plucked out by the roots, except a patch on the hinder part of the head, about twice the bigness of a crown-piece, which is ornamented with beads, feathers, wampum, stained deers hair, and such like baubles" (24). British newspapers confirmed this observation during the 1762 visit. "Their faces are painted a copper colour, and their heads are adorned with shells, feathers, ear-rings, and other trifling ornaments" (2007, 132n166).

A generation later, a Cherokee woman said: "The men, in cutting their hair, always left the lock growing on the crown of the head, this was braided and hung down the back. It was called a 'coo-tlah'" (Kilpatrick, 191). This is the word for lid and may refer to the hair's appearance or to beliefs about one of the four souls exiting the body through this area upon death (Witthoft 1982). This piece of hair was ornamented. The combination of feathers, beads, deer hair, and so on was referred to as *usgwetsiwo*, literally "hat." The portrait of GvnaShotte in London shows him wearing a black ostrich feather plume in his hair. (See color illustrations.)

Here is another description of feathers worn on the head of a warrior: "The quill end of the feather was inserted into a short piece of cane tied to the tuft of hair on top of the head, so as to cause the feather to stand erect. This feather had as many red stripes across it, as the candidate had killed enemies" (Payne, vol. 2, 37). This feather was given during the ceremony when a warrior has achieved the rank of *asgayagvsda egwo*. This ceremony involved wearing special clothing of deerskin dyed red, a special pattern of body paint, and an eagle feather.

Feathers were also worn inserted into a band worn around the head. Note that this bore no resemblance to the feathered war bonnet of the Lakota, Cheyenne, and other tribes of the Great Plains. Bartram notes, "A very curious diadem or band, about four inches broad [or less] and ingeniously wrought or woven, and curiously decorated with stones, beads, wampum, porcupine quills, &c, encircles their temples, the front peak of which is embellished with a high waving plume, of crane or heron feathers" (Bartram 1995, 121). Bartram also mentioned seeing the young men at the Cherokee town of Cowee dressed for the ballplay dance in the townhouse with "high waving plumes in their diadems" (1998, 234).

Cherokee men also wore silk handkerchiefs and scarves tied on their heads. These were obtained through trade and were both plain and printed. They sometimes wore them tied close to their heads, smooth over the forehead and tied in back, as in a later portrait of George Lowery. (See color illustrations.) Cherokees also ornamented these with breast buckles (ring brooches). One Cherokee man was buried in the Overhill Towns with a headscarf bearing more than three hundred such brooches (Riggs, personal communication).

Although Cherokee hats are not often mentioned, "gold laced hats" and "laced hats" were frequently given to them as presents in Charleston and Williamsburg. These are the tricorner hats worn by Europeans in colonial times, embellished with gold trim around the edges. Although no portraits or written descriptions associate Cherokees with these hats, they may have worn them. Mohawk leader Hendrick Theyanoguin wears a British officers coat and laced tricorner hat in a portrait from 1755.

Jewelry

Cherokee jewelry in the 1700s—that is, ornaments worn on or attached to the body—included: earrings, earbobs, and ear wraps; gorgets of shell and silver; necklaces of glass beads; necklaces and woven collars of wampum; bracelets and armbands of copper, silver and wire; finger rings; nose rings; brooches; and medals. Jewelry further ornamented shirts, skirts, leggings, moccasins, and headscarves.

Cherokees continued to use traditional materials such as wampum, native gems, and shell beads in their jewelry. To this repertoire they added glass beads and silver. They became adept at working silver, having been remarkable coppersmiths in the Mississippian era, 900 AD—1600 AD, not long before this century. As with other aspects of their dress, they retained some traditional items and materials. At the same time, they used new materials to make things in their old patterns, such using round silver gorgets in place of round shell gorgets. When

"The Brave old Hendrick the great sachem or chief of the Mohawk Indians," This hand-tinted engraving was printed in London, 1755, based on a lost painting. Hendrick Theyanoguin fought as an ally of the British and was killed in the Battle of Lake George. He is wearing a laced hat, officers' coat and waistcoat, and ruffled shirt. He is holding wampum and an axe.

they made these, they engraved animals or birds as decoration, instead of using the insignia of King George or the colonies, which were represented on the gorgets given to the Cherokees. Instead of armbands of shell or woven materials, they began wearing silver armbands acquired as gifts or payments during war. They created their own armbands and wristbands of silver and engraved them with representations of birds, animals, and fish. They used European items in distinctly Cherokee ways, for example, using multiple breast buckles (ring brooches) as ornaments rather than as functional fasteners. They applied them to large handkerchiefs worn as headscarves, to the shoulders of shirts, to the front panels of women's wrap skirts, to matchcoats, and to moccasins. Another example of "Cherokeeizing" trade goods comes from the Overhill Towns, where a woman decorated her skirt by hanging thimbles around the edge, punctured at the top and suspended by a cord of plant fiber. They traded for items they liked, such as certain kinds and colors of trade beads. They used small glass beads in the same way that they had used shell beads, as described in chapter 10, on weaving. They did use a few European items as Europeans used them, wearing silver ear bobs in their ears and military crescent gorgets around their necks.

Earrings

Cherokee women pierced their earlobes and wore one or two earrings in each ear. The silver earbobs popular in Europe and the Indian trade have been found in the graves of Cherokee women buried in the 1700s in the Overhills. One woman at Toqua had two in each ear. *Degadlihado* was the Cherokee word for this particular style of earring (DeBrahm 1971). After about 1770, the large circular earrings with pierced open work designs were made by Cherokee silversmiths and were worn by men and women. Cherokees and other tribes used silver coins to make these. They hammered the coins into large, thin disks and then cut out elaborate geometrical designs.

In the mid-1700s, however, Cherokee men favored a much more drastic style of ornamenting their ears. They slit the cartilage away from the outer rim of the ear, wrapped it in silver wire, let it heal, and then decorated their ears with plumes, silver earrings, and more. When Louis-Philippe, later the King of France, traveled among the Cherokees in the 1790s, he observed: "The outer rim of the ear is always detached with an incision among them. They wrap it with tin and hang from it very long and heavy ear pendants. Also they often have a triangle or other dangler passed through the nasal septum. These ornaments are worn only by men" (Sturtevant 1978, 202). You can see these slit ears in the lithograph of the three Cherokees in London in 1762.

These two pairs of silver ball and cone earrings were found in the grave of a Cherokee woman at Toqua, dated to the eighteenth century. Women pierced their ears with one or two holes, while men often slit their ears, wrapped the extended cartilage with silver or lead, and adorned it with additional earrings. Courtesy of the Frank McClung Museum collection.

The ears are slit and stretched to an enormous size, putting the person who undergoes the operation to incredible pain, being unable to lie on either side for near forty days. To remedy this, they generally slit but one at a time; so soon as the patient can bear it, they are wound round with wire to expand them, and are adorned with silver pendants and rings, which they likewise wear at the nose. This custom does not belong originally to the Cherokees but taken by them from the Shawnese, or other northern nations. (Timberlake, 25)

Although these unusual stretched ears are clearly visible in the lithograph, the painters Sir Joshua Reynolds and Francis Parsons omitted them from their respective portraits of Ostenaco and GvnaShotte:

> *Other southeastern tribes wore their ears in this fashion as well. Although the same things are commonly alike used or disused, by males and females; yet they distinguish their sexes in as exact a manner as any civilized nation. The women bore small holes in the lobe of their ears for their rings, but the young heroes cut a hole round almost the extremity of both their ears, which, til healed, they stretch out with a large tuft of buffalo's wool mixt with bear's oil: then they twist as much small wire round as will keep them extended in that hideous form. This custom however is wearing off apace. (Adair, 20)*

Wampum Collars, Gorgets, and Necklaces

Wampum collars were long sashes woven in a circle with beads of white and purple wampum, or cylindrical glass beads in white and black or sometimes white and blue. As Timberlake remarked, "They that can afford it wear a collar of wampum, which are beads cutout of clam shells, a silver breast-plate, and bracelets on their arms and wrists of the same metal" (25). The sashes around the necks of the Cherokees in the 1762 lithograph may be wampum collars as well. Earlier collars were made of copper beaten into very thin even sheets.

Gorgets in ancient Cherokee times were made of stone carved into simple rectangular shapes and were worn around the neck. During the Mississippian period Cherokees shared artwork styles with other southeastern tribes and created circular shell gorgets, finely incised with designs. In the eighteenth century, a few shell gorgets were still being made. The British gorget evolved from a piece of medieval armor that protected the throat. It was crescent-shaped and British

Shell gorget from marine mollusk, eighteenth century. Approximately 2 ½ inches wide. This small, plain, shell gorget represents a continuation of Mississippian traditions and trade routes into the historic period. Courtesy of the Frank McClung Museum collection.

Cherokee brass neck collar and arm bands, eighteenth century. The neck collar is approximately 2 ¼ inches wide. Courtesy of the Tommy Beutell collection.

Silver gorget, eighteenth century. This round silver gorget is engraved with a heron or crane and may be an example of Cherokee silverwork. Courtesy of the Frank McClung Museum collection.

Glass beads, eighteenth century, from Over-hill towns. Includes rattlesnake bead, blue padres, and tubular cobalt bead. Photograph by Barbara R. Duncan. Courtesy of the Museum of the Cherokee Indian collection.

Brass tubular beads, eighteenth century. These follow the Mississippian tradition of copper beads made from thin sheets of worked metal. Brass from kettles was sometimes hammered into thinner sheets and made into ornaments. Courtesy of the Frank McClung Museum collection.

officers wore them. They were given to the Cherokees and other Indian allies as special gifts and were sometimes engraved. During the eighteenth century, the British began making silver gorgets that were round, for gifts to their Cherokee and other American Indian allies. These were engraved with a variety of designs, including "SC" for South Carolina, Virginia, and the King's Arms. Later in the 1700s, Cherokees began engraving their own silver gorgets with representations of fish, deer, and birds.

Men and women wore necklaces of beads. Glass trade beads had existed among the Cherokees since the time of Hernando DeSoto's expedition in 1540. Popular glass beads among the Cherokees included blue, white, and red rounded beads about one-eighth of an inch in diameter (known as pony beads or padres today), blue chevron beads, green chevron beads, red chevron beads, blue glass beads, blue and white striped beads, black and white "rattlesnake" beads, "white-heart" beads that are red on the outside, faceted blue beads (sometimes called Russian cobalt today), and more. Small black beads of a rounded cylindrical shape are also common in Cherokee archaeological sites. All of these glass beads were made in southern Europe and in Africa for trade around the world, from about 1500 through today. When William Bartram visited the Cowee townhouse in 1776, in the evening, waiting for the stickball dance to begin, he saw "Presently a company of girls, hand in hand, dressed in clean white robes and ornamented with beads, bracelets, and a profusion of gay ribbands" (1998, 234). During the eighteenth century, Cherokees still made cylindrical beads rolled from a thin sheet of copper, as they had done for centuries; these were sometimes made from brass kettles that were worn out.

Armbands, Wristbands, Bracelets, and Rings

The tradition of giving armbands or bracelets to warriors is found in many cultures at many times around the world, including the Montangnard people of the highlands of southeast Asia over the past centuries; the Vikings in north-

ern Europe about 400 AD–1200 AD; and other northern Europeans like the Angles and Saxons, whose torcs and armbands of gold and silver survive in buried "hoards" still being discovered today. As N. Jaye Frederickson confirms, "Various kinds of bands were worn by almost all Eastern Woodland Indians. Armbands, legbands, bracelets, and headbands were all common ornaments. They were made of thin sheets of silver of varying widths, with holes drilled at the ends for ties, thus making the pieces adjustable in size" (56).

Cherokee men who fought in Virginia, Pennsylvania, and the Ohio Valley on the side of the British and had killed or captured the most enemies were given gifts of silver armbands and silver gorgets. Some of these were plainly made while others had delicate cut edges and rocker engraving. In this style of engraving, a hand tool was repeatedly rocked back and forth to create designs, some with beveled edges. (See color illustrations.)

Rings

Adair offers the following description of southeastern Indians in general:

> The men and women in old times used such coarse diamonds, as their own hilly country produced, when each had a bit of stone fastened with a deer's sinew to the tying of their hair, their nose, ears, and maccaseenes: but from the time we supplied them with our European ornaments, they have used brass and silver ear-rings, and finger-rings. (202)

The wearing of earbobs and finger rings was common in many tribes. Finger rings of the eighteenth century were often simple circlets or rings with set stones. The Cherokees specifically wore many rings during this time, as the elders described later in the Payne manuscript: "Finger rings were common to both men and women" (Payne, vol. 2, 21).

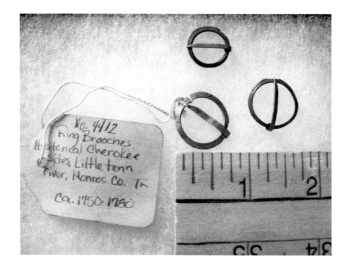

Pierced silver brooch from Great Tellico, 1700s. Silver. Courtesy of the Museum of the Cherokee Indian collection.

(*right*) Breast buckles from Great Tellico, 1700s. Silver. Courtesy of the Museum of the Cherokee Indian collection.

Brooches

The silver brooches worn by Cherokees of the eighteenth century varied in size and style. The most simple was the breast buckle or ring brooch, a circle about one inch in diameter with an attached piece that was used to pierce the cloth it attached to. Cloth was pulled up through the ring, pierced by the cross piece, and smoothed out. The same method of fastening was used on more elaborate brooches. Some were designs common in the "trade silver" of the time; this was first imported from Europe for the Indian trade and later made by silversmiths in Charleston, Williamsburg, and Philadelphia. Designs popular among the Cherokees included the council square or the "Luckenbooth" Scottish-style heart. Other brooches were circular with pierced work, made either by silversmiths of European descent or the Cherokees themselves.

Medals

Peace medals were given to many tribes, including the Cherokees, in addition to gorgets and armbands. In Cunne Shote's portrait, painted while he was in London in 1762, we can see he is wearing two medals, or medallions. One is a wedding medallion of King George III and Queen Charlotte, and the other is a Proclamation medal celebrating the king's coronation. These were likely presented to him while the Cherokee delegation was in London.

Among the peace medals given to the Cherokees was the only peace medal created by the state of Virginia. Thomas Jefferson gave these medals to the Cherokees at the end of the Revolutionary War, in 1780. The front was inscribed: "REBELLION TO TYRANTS IS OBEDIENCE TO GOD. VIRGINIA." The goddess Virtue with spear and sword is depicted standing on the figure of a tyrant. The obverse was inscribed "HAPPY WHILE UNITED." It shows an American Indian with a peace pipe and a man in eighteenth-century European dress sitting beneath a tree, with a harbor and three ships in the background. The round medal is surmounted with a wing and a pipe at the top. Ten silver medals and additional bronze medals were originally cast and distributed (Bradley, 2009). (See color illustrations.)

12 *1800s, 1900s, 2000s*

This final chapter explores how Cherokee clothing has changed since the 1700s. It provides some context for the clothing of that century. Subsequent centuries also show how clothing continued to reflect the changing political, cultural, and physical environment. Cherokee people continue to draw from both traditional styles and materials and new ideas to create clothing that expresses their identity.

civilization policy

Trail of Tears

east and west

twentieth century

ribbon shirts and tear dresses

twenty-first century and

   revitalization

The 1800s

After the Revolutionary War, the Cherokee nation reached a low point. Their alliance with the British led the new American government to burden them with punitive expeditions and treaties. General Griffith Rutherford led an expedition to "extirpate" the Cherokees in the fall of 1776. Thirty-six towns were destroyed that year: people killed, crops and orchards burned, houses razed. Only some towns were rebuilt. People had to eat their horses to survive. A smallpox epidemic in 1785 killed between 30 and 50 percent of the population. The Treaty of Hopewell in 1785 transferred large amounts of land to the new United States of America. Previously established trade relationships were gone. Dragging Canoe and the Chickamauga Cherokees fought for Cherokee land and sovereignty from 1776 through 1794, maintaining their land and independence in southeastern Tennessee and northern Alabama. But with Dragging Canoe's death in 1792, followed by the Treaty of Tellico Blockhouse in 1794, peace was finally made. Even the violent, much-feared Doublehead ceased making war and became a businessman for the rest of his life.

By 1800 many changes had affected Cherokees. They had allied with the American government rather than with the European nations and colonies. They had lost many of their towns with their traditional houses and canebrakes, and families had moved to log cabins and smaller settlements. They began to follow the so-called civilization policy, as stated in letters and speeches by George Washington and Thomas Jefferson. Between 1785 and 1835 the Cherokees transformed themselves into a thriving nation within the larger nation of the United States.

Cherokee clothing reflected these changes. The warrior fashion and feather capes of the eighteenth century gave way to clothing that covered both men and women in yards of cloth; Cherokee men wore turbans and jackets, and women wore long skirts and shawls. Within the existing choices of materials and styles, Cherokee men and women once again created clothing that reflected their identities.

Often Cherokees wore combinations of old and new styles according to their preferences and the materials available to them. Some completely adopted European-American clothing, such as political leaders doing business in Washington or those who were students in missionary schools. Some Cherokees wore older styles to affirm their connection with the past and with older Cherokee traditions during this time of many changes.

Part of the civilization policy mandated that Cherokee men give up hunting and "learn to" farm and that Cherokee women "learn to" spin and weave. The agenda of the federal government was for Cherokee men to give up hunting so that millions of acres claimed as hunting grounds would become available to land speculators. As we know, Cherokees had been cultivating plants for thousands of years; soldiers as recently as the Revolutionary War, in 1776, complained what hard work it was to destroy all the Cherokee orchards and fields in their towns. Cherokee women had been spinning and weaving for more than 9,500 years. Nonetheless, during this period, the ability of Cherokee women to spin, weave, and wear yards of cloth became a measure of their "civilization." Indian agents at Springplace (near present-day Chatsworth, Georgia) and Tellico Blockhouse (near present-day Vonore, Tennessee) distributed spinning wheels, cards for processing wool, looms, and plows. Also at these locations they provided instruction in spinning, weaving, farming, and blacksmithing.

In a letter to Secretary of War Albert Gallatin on February 27, 1826, John Ridge described the laws, customs, architecture, and changing habits of the Cherokees. He presented a portrait of a progressive group of people, and clothing is very much a part of his evidence. Note that in the passage below, by "domestic," he means made in the home.

Domestic manufactures is still confined to women who were first prevailed to undertake it. These consist of white or striped homespun, coarse woolen blankets & in many instances very valuable & comfortable, twilled & figured coverlets. Woolen & cotton stockings are mostly manufactured for domestic use within the nation. I can only say that their domestic cloths are preferred by us to those brought from New England. Domestic plaids our people are most generally clothed with them, but calicoes, silks, cambrics, &c, handkerchiefs & shawls &c are introduced by Native merchants, who generally trade to Augusta in Georgia.... Cherokees on the Tennessee River have already

*commenced to trade in cotton & grow the article in large plantations and
they have realized very handsome profit.*

Moravian missionaries at Springplace and Congregationalist missionaries at
the Brainerd School (in present-day Chattanooga, Tennessee) documented their
students' changes in clothing as proof of their conversion to Christianity. For
the missionaries, becoming Christian meant becoming "civilized," which meant
living as white people in New England did. Clothing was one indicator of this.
Take, for example, the following entry in the *Brainerd Journal* (Phillips and Phillips 1998, 50–51):

> *April 9, 1818 a Cherokee woman, mother of one of our boys & very decent
> in her appearance, called on us for the first time. Being dressed neatly in
> the fashion of our country women ~~called Christian~~ [sic] we hoped she had
> obtained from white people some knowledge of our God & Savior as well as of
> our manners & dress.*

Throughout the *Brainerd Journal* and *Springplace Diaries* (McClinton 2007),
gifts of clothing, cloth, and blankets from Christians around the country are
recorded. The missionaries seemed to regard these gifts as part of delivering the
gospel, as well as of making the Cherokees resemble them in dress:

> *Oct. 13, 1819 Five boxes of clothing came on from Knoxville by way of Bal-
> timore. . . . We ought to be very grateful to that God . . . for putting it into
> the hearts of his dear children to send, from the most remote parts of the
> U.S. these seasonable supplies of ready made clothing to cover these naked
> children of the forest; & in this way to evince the power & excellence of that
> gospel which he has commanded to be preached to every creature. (Phillips
> and Phillips 1998, 133–134).*

In describing the conversion of Catherine Brown, a young Cherokee woman,
missionaries gave equal importance to changes in her style of dress as to her
ability to read the Bible. They praised the fact that after her conversion her appearance mirrored that of any young woman in New England: "[When she first
came to us] she was vain, and excessively fond of dress, wearing a profusion of
ornaments in her ears. . . . Since she became religious, her trinkets have gradually
disappeared, till only a single drop remains in each ear. She can now read well in
the Bible" (Anderson 1831, 30–32).

The adoption of European clothing represented the acceptance of "civilization"
and Christianity; conversely, the rejection of those styles represented, for some
Cherokee people, their loyalty to older, essentially Cherokee traditions. During
the Cherokee ghost dance movement, from 1811 to 1813, people burned clothing
and other items that came from European-Americans to show their rejection of
that culture. White Path also led a movement that embraced older, traditional
Cherokee values, and his followers wore the older clothing styles as well.

The census conducted by the United States in 1835 noted how many spinners
and weavers each household contained. It documented a total of 4,129 spinners

Tah-Chee, Dutch, (d. 1848) a Cherokee leader of the early 1800s, wearing turban, feather, linen shirt, cravat, coat of printed material, and fingerwoven sash. From McKenney and Hall, 1837.

Major Ridge, Nunna Hidihi (ca. 1770–1839) a warrior, council member, fullblood, and traditionalist, wearing formal European-American clothing. From McKenney and Hall, 1837. After a portrait by Charles Bird King. Courtesy of the Museum of the Cherokee Indian collection.

and 1,460 weavers. That means that about one in four people could spin and about one in ten people could weave (*1835 Cherokee Census* 2002, 66). If we assume that women were the spinners and weavers, and that women made up half the population, then one in two women could spin, and one in five women could weave. (Note that in order for a woman to weave for an hour, other women must spin for several hours.) The census also documented the number of people who could read and write English or Cherokee, how many buildings were present and their kind, acres under cultivation, fruit trees, and so on.

During the time leading up to Removal in 1838, Cherokee men wore a wide variety of clothing styles. Some still wore parts of the traditional dress of the 1700s: breechclout, leggings, linen shirt, and moccasins. Leggings were simplified, with the seam moved to the front and no decorated flaps on the sides. To this ensemble was added a turban, a length of printed or solid cloth loosely wound about the head and extending above the head for several inches. The height of the turban seems to be a matter of individual preference or perhaps of the length of cloth used. Cherokee men also adapted a style that they had avoided in the 1700s: a long coat with capes over the shoulders. In the 1700s, Cherokees associated this "hunting coat" with white men who lived in the backwoods and had adopted this as part of their American style of dress. Because these men

Buckskin coat with silk ribbon, 1830, Eastern Cherokee. Photo by Kristy Maney Herron. Courtesy of the National Museum of the American Indian collection.

were often encroaching on Cherokee land, Cherokees didn't want to look like them. After 1800, though, boundaries were solidified, problems changed, and Cherokee people began making and wearing these coats in buckskin and other materials. Some were embroidered or decorated with piping of trade cloth. Men also wore a softly shaped coat with a rolled collar, about mid-thigh in length, in plain, striped, or patterned material. These coats were often fastened with elaborate fingerwoven beaded belts. They continued to wear bags, although the style of these changed.

A transitional style of beadwork in the late 1700s and early 1800s employed lines and panels of white beads appliquéd on sashes of navy trade cloth, sometimes with red cloth also sewn on, surrounded with lines and panels of white beads, as in this example from the Museum of the Cherokee Indian. Other southeastern tribes, notably the Choctaw, made these too, and for them this style continued throughout the 1800s.

Colored glass beads became widely available after 1800, because of changes in manufacturing technology in Europe. Cherokee beadwork styles changed from lines of single, white glass beads applied in geometric designs to panels of colored beads applied in designs of flowers, animals, and scrolls. These were beaded onto moccasins, bags, and straps. The bags, known as "bandolier bags," became very beautiful and elaborate among the Cherokees

David Vann portrait from McKenney and Hall, after a painting by Charles Bird King. Note his silk cravat, ruffled linen shirt, coat, and strap made by fingerweaving with beads. Courtesy of the Museum of the Cherokee Indian collection.

Cherokee sash, ca. 1820. Navy wool with red wool applique and white glass beads, unknown thread. Courtesy of the Museum of the Cherokee Indian collection.

(*right*) Bandolier bag, wool, cotton, glass beads. Created by Dagwa, the Whale, in 1846 in Tahlequah and presented by him to American Lt. Cave Johnson Couts. Courtesy of the Collection of the Gilcrease Museum, Tulsa, Oklahoma.

and other southeastern tribes. One covered with elaborate beading was given as a present from Sam Houston to Andrew Jackson. Another was given as a present from a Cherokee warrior in Indian Territory to a U.S. Army officer in 1846 to show his esteem and appreciation. Because these bags evolved from the shot pouch or necessary bag, they continued to be associated with warriors. Note that the presents above were between military leaders.

Of the eight portraits made of Cherokee leaders and published in 1838 by McKenney and Hall, half show the leaders in the new Cherokee style of dress,

with turban, soft coat, and fingerwoven belt with beads. These include Tachee (Dutch), Spring Frog, Sequoyah, and David Vann, although Vann is not wearing a turban. The other four portraits show Cherokee leaders in the formal clothes worn by Americans: Major Ridge, John Ridge, and John Ross, of whom there are two portraits. An additional portrait of George Lowery by Catlin about this time shows him wearing much older traditional dress: a head scarf lies flat on his head, his ears are slit, and he wears large round silver earrings with pierced designs, a silver gorget, and a white linen shirt, all in the late-eighteenth-century style. (See color illustrations.)

During the time period from about 1800 to 1840, Cherokee clothing for men and women underwent radical changes. A new style of Cherokee men's traditional dress was created that incorporated elements of the old style, such as leggings, sashes, and moccasins, but added new coats and headgear, creating a different profile for Cherokee men. The clothing of Cherokee women also changed radically during this time period, from the knee-length skirts of the 1700s to ankle-length skirts, blouses, and shawls, so that the women became almost entirely covered in cloth. If some Cherokee women maintained an older, freer style, there is little evidence of it.

The Cherokee Removal between 1838 and 1839 had a profound impact on all Cherokees. After the Removal, Cherokee people maintained communities in the southern Appalachians and in Arkansas, and they created new communities in Indian Territory. Cherokee people in the Southeast struggled for fifty years to establish a legal identity as the Eastern Band of Cherokee Indians, buying back their original homeland piece by piece and finally achieving federal recognition

(*above, left*) "Ah-hee-te-wah-chee, a pretty woman in civilized dress," by George Catlin. In his color print of this Cherokee woman, she is wearing a green blouse with white stripes and a red shawl with pink flowers. Her hair appears to have gray in it. Probably painted at Fort Gibson in 1834. "Pretty Woman" was a Cherokee war title used like "Beloved Woman." This drawing has been incorrectly identified as Nancy Ward (Catlin, 1842, vol. 2, 119).

(*above, right*) Spring Frog (ca. 1754) portrait from McKenney and Hall, 1837. He was born near Chickamauga Creek and was a stickball player. He is wearing a turban, ruffled linen shirt, soft coat, and fingerwoven belt with beads.

Qweti (Betty) and child, from the Eastern Band of Cherokee Indians, ca. 1880. Note her handwoven shawl. Photo by James Mooney. Courtesy of the Museum of the Cherokee Indian collection and National Anthropological Archives.

Eastern Band Cherokee women at stickball game, ca. 1880. Babies are still carried on women's backs, tied with a length of cloth. Woman is wearing hand-carved wooden comb in her hair. Women wore extra layers of clothing to ball games and wagered their clothing. Photo by James Mooney. Courtesy of the Museum of the Cherokee Indian collection and National Anthropological Archives.

Eastern Band Cherokee women at stickball game, ca. 1880. They are wearing kerchiefs, dresses, shawls, and aprons. Little boys are dressed like men in suit coats, shirts, and trousers. Photo by James Mooney. Courtesy of the Museum of the Cherokee Indian collection and National Anthropological Archives.

in 1868 and legal standing as a state corporation in 1889. (Members of the Eastern Band were recognized as United States citizens by a special act of Congress in 1930.)

By the late 1800s, Cherokee clothing in the southern Appalachians resembled that of their white neighbors in many respects; but a Cherokee version of that style still existed. Some Cherokee men still wore moccasins and turbans, and occasionally leggings. Stickball players wore brief, lightweight homemade shorts for the game, with appliquéd stars indicating their ranks. Cherokee women spun and wove cloth and wore handmade shawls, as well as kerchiefs on their heads. They carried their babies tied to their backs with a length of cloth as they had done for many generations.

The 1900s

The changes of the twentieth century are reflected in Cherokee clothing. At the beginning of the century Cherokees wore their best clothing in their graduation portraits from the Cherokee Boarding School: beautiful handmade dresses for young women and handmade suits for young men. In 1910, Rev. Armstrong Cornsilk wore an old-style turban with a suit coat at the dedication of the Junaluska gravesite in Robbinsville, North Carolina. Cherokee boys and girls wore the military uniforms of the Carlisle Indian School and other boarding schools, where they were sent. Cherokee men and women wore military uniforms and nurses' uniforms in World War I, World War II, Korea, Vietnam, and Desert Storm. Cherokees wore mid-century "American" dress in snapshots sent home from cities during the Relocation era of the mid-twentieth century. Jimi Hendrix claimed African and Cherokee descent and paid homage to both cultures in the style of his psychedelic clothing. Beginning in the 1960s and 1970s, Cherokee people created elaborate regalia for dancing at powwow competitions. In the 1970s, they wore ribbon shirts and tear dresses to symbolize their identity. "Chiefs" educated the public wearing Plains headdresses on the streets of Cherokee, North Carolina. Cherokee students wore graduation gowns and mortarboards with beaded edges and eagle feathers. Throughout the century, Cherokee grandmothers wore housedresses and head scarves and carried white-oak basket purses. Finally everyone wore blue jeans, T-shirts, and sneakers.

The last memories of spinning and weaving with native plants passed away with Molly Runningwolf Sequoyah during the 1970s. She remembered how to spin thread on her thigh as her mother had done in order to make shrouds from dogbane (*Apocynum androsaemifolium*) (Witthoft 1983). The last knowledge of making fingerwoven belts with beads woven in and long ties with beads passed away with the last weaver, Mary Shell, in the 1990s.

At the turn of the twentieth century, boarding schools took children away from their families and communities to prevent them from being Indian. School authorities took away children's clothes and cut their hair, giving them uniforms and short American hairstyles instead. These changes symbolized the destruction of their identity as American Indians. Cherokee children were forcibly sent to the Carlisle Indian School in Pennsylvania; the Hampton School in Virginia;

Dedication ceremony at Junaluska gravesite, Robbinsville, North Carolina, 1910. Reverend Armstrong Cornsilk (standing at right) is wearing a turban, one of the last times this appears among Eastern Cherokees. Courtesy of the Museum of the Cherokee Indian collection.

and the Chillocco boarding school in Oklahoma. Even in the town of Cherokee, North Carolina, a boarding school kept children away from their families for most of the year. They were beaten if they spoke Cherokee language. This school operated from 1893 until 1948. The Bureau of Indian Affairs continued to operate the Cherokee school system until 1990, and Cherokee culture was not part of the curriculum.

After World War II, powwows became popular intertribal gatherings. Beautiful regalia was made specifically for each dance, and each outfit required many hours of sewing, beadwork, leatherwork, and featherwork. Several family members might work together to create the items needed for one person to wear to dance. Individuals waited years to legally acquire eagle feathers to make bustles. The specific powwow dances came primarily from western tribes. These included the men's northern traditional dance, a war dance from the Great Plains; the fancy dance; and the grass dance. Dances specifically for women included the shawl dance and jingle dress dance. Throughout the United States and Canada, powwows provided a public place for American Indian people and First Nations people to get together and socialize, share their culture, compete in dances, and meet the public. Powwow dance competitions used the same basic repertoire of dances in every location.

Throughout the twentieth century, a stereotypical public image of American Indians was created: first by Wild West shows, then traveling medicine shows, then silent films, followed by television and movies. War bonnets and fringe featured prominently, as they do in today's sports mascots and offensive Halloween costumes.

But in the 1970s, real American Indian people came into the public eye through their part in civil rights activism, events at Wounded Knee, and finally the celebration of multicultural America during the Bicentennial. About this time, some new clothing styles also affirmed Indian identity: ribbon shirts for men and tear dresses for Cherokee women.

Ribbon shirts, like powwow regalia, were worn by men of all tribes, and some men still wear them. They consist of a long sleeved shirt handmade of solid or printed cloth, with bands of ribbons sewn horizontally across the shoulders in the back and across the chest in the front. Vertical ribbon strips are added along the outside of the torso, along with ribbon strips around the cuffs and collar. Some ribbon shirts also feature extra lengths of ribbon flowing freely from the ends of the appliquéd ribbon. The ribbon is usually narrow, from about one-eighth of an inch to no more than half an inch wide. These stripes of ribbon evoke the fascination with ribbon decoration that was so prevalent in the 1700s. Shirt fabrics vary from plain colors and calico flowered prints to American Indian–themed prints. The shirts are usually worn with jeans and moccasins or boots. Often bolo ties with beaded rosettes are worn as well, or "choker" necklaces of bone hairpipes. (See photo of Michell Hicks with Warriors of AniKituhwa at Cowee.)

The beaded rosette bolo is the twentieth-century incarnation of the gorget, in this author's opinion. Gorgets evolved from the stone rectangles of the Archaic period, to the carved shell disks of the Mississippian period, to the silver disks of the 1700s, and finally to the beaded rosettes of the twentieth century. All are labor intensive, highly valued, and worn around the neck.

People from different tribes continued their own clothing traditions to some extent throughout the twentieth century. For example, Seminole and Micosukee people made colorful patchwork and appliquéd skirts, shirts, and vests. Choctaw people made clothing with rows of appliquéd diamonds honoring the rattlesnake. Anishinabe people continued traditions of moose hide with quillwork and beadwork. Navaho women wore velvet blouses, broomstick gathered skirts, distinctive moccasins, and beautiful silver jewelry in the Navaho style. Apache people had their own moccasin designs and clothing styles. Tribes of the Pacific northwest coast continued traditions of cedar-bark woven hats and aprons. Inuit people, Hawai'ian people, and others continued elements of traditional dress, if only as ceremonial dress and dance regalia or worn by some elders.

In the 1970s, Cherokee women turned to the tear dress. Made of rectangles of calico cloth with gussets under the sleeves (in the manner of eighteenth-century shirts), the tear dress was gathered below a shoulder yoke, at the waist, and at an additional ruffle about mid-calf. It was also gathered to fit at the wrists. Appliqués of cloth triangles represented the mountains left behind in the Southeast. Decorative rows of ribbon and panels of geometric shapes also adorned this style of dress, and Cherokee seamstresses were creative in their combinations of fabrics and colors. A legend said that this dress was patterned after a dress found in a trunk that had come from the mountains of Georgia to Oklahoma on the Trail of Tears. It was called a tear dress, and the "tear" was pronounced either like the result of weeping, because of its association with the Trail of Tears, or like the ripping motion used to create the rectangles of cloth. The legend stated that the cloth was ripped because the Cherokee women didn't have scissors. (See illustration of scissors from the 1700s in chapter 2.) This was designated as the official dress of the Cherokee Nation of Oklahoma. It became very popular as a symbol of Cherokee identity and American Indian identity. Some Cherokee people, including the Miss Cherokees of the Cherokee Nation and the members of the Cherokee National Youth Choir, still wear it today.

Although this dress became a powerful symbol and is still part of the wardrobe of many Cherokee women, this style of dress was not worn by Cherokee women before 1970. When Virginia Stroud was Cherokee Tribal Princess, she wore a Kiowa buckskin dress. When she won the Miss Indian America title in 1970, she wanted a Cherokee dress to wear. Her mother and her mother's friends put together their heads, their imaginations, and their sewing machines, and in a late night session in Tahlequah created the first Cherokee tear dress. Don Stroud and Margaret Raymond were there when this happened, and shared this story. Their mothers were among the seamstresses (Raymond 2006–07; Stroud 2006–07).

Ribbon shirts and tear dresses became symbols of Cherokee identity in the late twentieth century. They were worn proudly by people at special events and at powwows. They were sewn for children. They appeared, and still appear, on dolls and in artwork. They served the purpose of creating a visible Cherokee identity that was different from mainstream American and western Plains Indians stereotypes.

Footwear at this time included moccasins and cowboy boots. Jewelry included beadwork rosettes as bolo ties and belt buckles. Necklaces and earrings were made from glass beads, porcupine quills, and "corn beads." These natural beads, also called Job's tears, have a Trail of Tears legend associated with them. Men and women wore fingerwoven belts and leather belts. Silver jewelry from southwestern tribes like the Navaho and Zuni was also popular among Cherokee people who could afford it or traded for it. Pendleton blankets from Oregon were used to make coats and vests. Women who wanted a traditional Cherokee purse carried a white-oak basket purse. Once again, Cherokee people created a style of dress out of old patterns and new ideas, from materials gathered and traded, with inspiration from other tribes and from their imaginations, and stamped their identity upon it.

The 2000s

This book is about Cherokee clothing in the 1700s, with earlier millennia and later centuries added for context. But this book came about only because of the revitalization of Cherokee clothing in the early twenty-first century. Cherokee people, starting with the Warriors of AniKituhwa, became interested in knowing more about their history, their culture, their dances, and their clothing from earlier periods.

The early 2000s also saw the beginnings of a cultural renaissance among the Eastern Cherokee and other tribes. In 1997 and 2008 the Eastern Band bought back the Kituhwa Mound and the Cowee Mound. In addition to buying back sacred places, the Eastern Cherokee and others renewed their efforts to maintain their traditions, their natural resources, and their languages. In 2004 the

National Museum of the American Indian opened in Washington, D.C., giving American Indian tribes a visible national presence.

Traditions change with every generation. People keep what is meaningful to them, in their time and place. We pass what we value most to our children and grandchildren. Sometimes to make our traditions meaningful we reach back even farther in time.

This is what Cherokee people in the Eastern Band are doing, as they reach back to a time when the Cherokees were a world power, negotiating with Britain, France, Spain, the colony of Virginia, and the colony of South Carolina, and with other tribes in the eighteenth century. They are adding items of clothing, techniques of making clothing, and styles from that period back into a style of dress that reclaims a time of strength and creativity, as well as a time of survival in the face of adversity.

Let me note here an important difference between history and tradition. If Cherokee people want to recreate historical clothing, for presentations at the Museum of the Cherokee Indian, the Oconaluftee Indian Village, Colonial Williamsburg, or Fort Necessity National Battlefield, they now have the information to do so. They have mastered the skills and found the necessary materials. They can dress exactly as Cherokees did in 1750, or 1770, down to the exact size of the beads on their fingerwoven garters, the color of their matchcoats, and the style of their earrings. And when they do so, they *are* Cherokee people, the descendants of Ostenaco, and Attakullakulla, and the Beloved women of Chota, and Dragging Canoe, who wore this same style of clothing while negotiating with and while fighting with the British, the French, and the Americans. They are not re-enactors in "redface." They are Cherokee people representing their own history. This style can be described as "historical" clothing.

But if Cherokee people want to take this information and use it to revitalize and continue those traditions, then they are not making historical clothing. They are continuing their own traditions of clothing, expressing themselves in ways that are pleasing and meaningful to them, as they pass these revitalized traditions to the next generation. Using clothing to represent history and changing clothing to continue tradition are both important aspects of self-expression and cultural expression. These changes and individual expressions should be described as "in the Cherokee tradition."

Here are some of the ways this has been happening. The Warriors of Ani-Kituhwa led the way. After research in the winter of 2005, they and I, through the Museum of the Cherokee Indian, offered workshops in making moccasins, leggings, and clothing such as shirts, breechclouts, skirts, and matchcoats. By the fall of 2005 they dressed in historically accurate clothing to present programs at Colonial Williamsburg. The next spring, Brenda Rousseau from Colonial Williamsburg's clothing design department traveled as a volunteer to Cherokee, North Carolina, to demonstrate how to tailor eighteenth-century shirts. After this workshop, Nancy Maney and her sister Johnnie Ruth Maney became shirt makers and clothing makers. Several employees of the Oconaluftee Indian Village also took this workshop and began improving the accuracy of the historical clothing at the Village. A new production of "Unto These Hills" outdoor drama also incorporated this new research on historical clothing.

In the spring of 2006 the Museum of the Cherokee Indian and I set up a tour for the Warriors of AniKituhwa in northeast Oklahoma. They danced at a conference in Tulsa, in seven public schools where Cherokee children were students, and in public programs at the Cherokee Nation complex. The men of the group also provided workshops on how to sing and lead Cherokee traditional social and animal dances, while the author provided workshops on making eighteenth-century clothing at the Cherokee Nation complex. We repeated this tour and these workshops in the spring of 2007.

Also in 2006, the Museum of the Cherokee Indian opened the exhibit "Emissaries of Peace: the 1762 Cherokee and British Delegations," a We the People exhibit sponsored by the National Endowment for the Humanities, the Cherokee Preservation Foundation, Harrah's Foundation, First Citizens Bank, and The Cannon Foundation. This exhibit shows the contrasting Cherokee and British worldviews of the eighteenth century, based on the *Memoirs* of Henry Timberlake. It uses artwork, artifacts, video, audio, and life-size figures to tell the story. Among the artifacts are many examples of clothing, jewelry, and weapons of the period. This exhibit became very popular, traveled to four other venues, and was seen by more than two million people, in North Carolina, Tennessee, Oklahoma, and Washington, D.C. It also became the basis for an Electronic Field Trip and documentary drama coproduced with Colonial Williamsburg. The exhibit was the impetus for Cherokee events in six states and a series of publications by the Museum and the University of North Carolina Press, including this book. The exhibit has also served as a way to showcase artifacts that the community can continue to learn from.

Within the Eastern Band, several institutions have responded to people's interest in revitalizing clothing with styles from the 1700s. The Museum of the Cherokee Indian has led the way. The Cherokee Historical Association and Oconoluftee Indian Village portray a village of 1750 and have revised their clothing with this new information. They have also added a station where Karen George is fingerweaving with beads. The pageant committee for the Miss Cherokees formally adopted Cherokee clothing of the 1700s as the standard for contestants, with a resolution by Tribal Council.

The Museum of the Cherokee Indian has sponsored workshops on making feather capes; making nets; fingerweaving with beads; making moccasins; making shirts; twining fabric and skirts; and making other clothing of the 1700s. The Museum is also the official sponsor of the Warriors of AniKituhwa. Using research conducted at the request of Cherokee women, the author commissioned the first feather cape on a netted base, which was created by Deborah Harding of the Carnegie Museum of Natural History in Pittsburgh, and that cape is part of the Emissaries of Peace exhibit. Harding has continued to be a partner in the process of revitalization and has shared her knowledge of fingerweaving with beads in the diagonal interlacing style in several workshops at the Museum. The Museum has also offered workshops with Harding on how to make net-

Miss Cherokees at Colonial Williamsburg, 2010. Emma Stamper, Little Miss Cherokee; Kaley Locust, Junior Miss Cherokee; Annie Cedilla, Teen Miss Cherokee; Tonya Carroll, Miss Cherokee. Photo by Barbara R. Duncan.

ting, feather capes, and most recently, twined-weft weaving of Cherokee cloth. In 2014 the author and Harding teamed up to create reproductions of the Clifty Creek skirt and of ancient, indigenous Cherokee cloth.

Since the Warriors' interest in the traditions of the 1700s began, they and others have mastered various techniques. They have learned to make their own moccasins and clothing. Richard Saunooke has been making wampum belts. Antonio Grant has been doing shell carving, creating shell gorgets; he also has learned to do porcupine quill work. Kody Grant has learned the several braiding methods to make prisoner ties, an essential item for eighteenth-century warriors. Karen George has become a master of diagonal interlacing, the oblique finger-weaving with beads, working with wool and with buffalo hair, creating belts and garters in the eighteenth-century style. Several women have made feather capes for their daughters, nieces, and granddaughters competing in the Miss Cherokee

Micah Swimmer and his son Ogana, in 2010 at Southeast Tribes Festival. Photo by Shan Goshorn.

Malia Davis and Connor McCoy dressed for "Heroes Day" at Cherokee Elementary School, 2008. Malia's hero was Kara Martin, Miss Cherokee. Connor's hero was Sequoyah. Photo by Rosie McCoy.

pageants. They have decorated their wrap skirts with silk ribbon from China, trade silver brooches, cylindrical wampum beads, bells, and dangling thimbles. The Museum continues to offer workshops in making eighteenth-century clothing.

Miss Cherokees of all ages have been wearing wrap skirts and leggings, trade silver, and feather capes. Using the research of the author, the resources of Colonial Williamsburg, and the sewing expertise and creativity of Nancy Maney and Johnnie Ruth Maney, these young women have elaborated on "bodices" and "short gowns" to make these tops. They have also been wearing shifts and chemises as summer dresses, like the laughing girls William Bartram described in the Cowee townhouse more than two centuries ago. They have brought beauty and elegance to these styles as well as bringing them back to life.

The Warriors of AniKituhwa and the Miss Cherokees have been models for advertising campaigns for Cherokee, creating a new public image for the tribe. They are inspiring young Cherokee people.

As always, clothing has meaning, and the revitalization of "traditional" clothing based on information from the 1700s has become a source of interest and pride for Cherokee people. Cherokee women are once again weaving with natural fibers, making feather capes, and creating beaded belts and garters with diagonal interlacing in the eighteenth-century style, and Cherokee men are wearing breechclouts and leggings, linen shirts and matchcoats, wampum collars, and brain-tanned moccasins. The changing styles of Cherokee clothing are a symbol of the efforts of Cherokee people to reclaim their past and their strength as they move into the future.

Appendix A: Glossary of Cherokee Words
Related to Clothing

This list provides words in Cherokee language related to clothing and adornment common in the eighteenth century. Some of these words are still in use while others have been lost, either because the items of clothing have become archaic or because of language loss during the mid- to late twentieth century. Words for actions such as weaving, sewing, winding, putting clothes on, taking clothes off, and so on are still in use.

These words come from the word lists and dictionaries of Gerard DeBrahm (1756), Daniel Butrick and David Brown (1819), James Mooney, assisted by Will West Long (1900), Duane King (1975), and Durbin Feeling and William Pulte (1975). Words from Mooney and Long were collected from elders, some of whom were born about 1800 or earlier. These words were obtained from Manuscript 351 held by the National Anthropological Archives and also available in digital form at the Museum of the Cherokee Indian, Documenting Endangered Languages project.

The words are spelled using English phonetics as standardized in the printed Cherokee syllabary chart from 1828. This is the most commonly used orthography today (Bender 2003). Words are provided in their full form. In conversational usage today, syllables might be dropped or contracted.

Pronunciation of consonants is as in English. Pronunciation of vowels is as follows:

a as in father
e as in able
i as in see
o as in open
u as in prove
v as in uh, pronounced nasally.

English	Cherokee	literal meaning	source
adornment on top of man's head	alsgwetuwo	hat	df, db
	guhlvdi	also pronounced "coodla"—lid	df, w
apron	atsesado		df, dk eastern
armband of silver	adela haliloglohi		db
bareheaded, closely shaved	uskwaluga	uska = head, skull	jm351
barefoot	nulasvdlv'i		jm351
bead	adela	bead, money	
belt	adadlosdi	Western Cherokee dialect	df
	adatsosdi	Eastern Cherokee dialect	dk
blanket	tsvsgwanvni		jm ms351
blanket, striped	tsusgwanvni		jm
bracelets	dilihedlohi		
braid, he or she is braiding or making rope	asdeyoha		
breechclout	diseldi		jm
breechclout belt	adadlosdi	same as belt	jm
buttons	diktoli	eyes	db
checked shirt	utuesdi ahnawo		
cloth or shirt	ahnawo		df ,dk
clothing	dihnawo		bu
coat	gasaleni		df
earbobs	degadlihado	Western Cherokee dialect	db
	degatsihado	Eastern Cherokee dialect	
earrings (modern)	adliado		df
earrings (eastern dialect)	adliyvda		jm351
feather	ugidali		df, dk
feather headdress	tsugidvlididitsa		jm351
fringe	gadaluyadv'i		jm351
garters, pair	dinidlosdi		jm
garter, sing.	anidlosdi		jm
garters, Indian	digwetso		db
gorget	adanedasdla		jm351
handkerchief	adlogi		db
	ayatsohi		jt, dk
hide, skin of animal with hair on	ganegaldi		
hide, raw	utso		db
hide, dressed, deer	utsowodi		db, jm351
hide, elk	awi egwa ganeka	big deer hide	jm351
hide, rabbit	tsistu ganeka	rabbit hide	jm351
hide, beaver	doyv ganeka	beaver hide	jm351
hide, otter	tsiyu ganeka	otter hide (otter same word as poplar, canoe, airplane)	jm351
jacket	ahnuwo sgwalohi		db
lace	adela	same as bead, money	db
leather	ganotsi		
leggings, pair of	dilsgvlatvli		jm ms351

English	Cherokee	literal meaning	source
leggings or shoe boots	dasigiyagi	shoe boots—person's name	jm
linen, striped	tsulaledi		db
	tsuloldi	striped	df
match coat, mantle	ahnawo utana	cloth, it grew big	db
mirror, looking glass	adakehdi		db, df
moccasins	ulasulo	moccasin—same word became used as modern shoe	jm
moccasins, pair	tsvtsawodi	pair of moccasins	jm ms351
naked	uyelaha'i		jm351
necklace	ahyetla		jm351
needle	yvgi	same word as fork, nail	db, df
paint	disuhwisdi	the paint itself	
paint, clay	wohodi	traditional reddish brown paint	db, jm
paint, black	gvnige'I wodi	black paint	jm351
paint, red	wodige'I wodi	paint-colored-paint	jm351
paint, yellow	dalonige'I wodi	yellow paint	jm351
pants, breeches	asulo		
petticoat	asano		db, jt
pocket	adlawadv'i or tsawata	atsowata	jm351
pouch	ayasvda		jm351
ribbon	agwelosdi	part in hair	db
ring	aliyesvsdawa		jm351
scissors	dilsdoyhdi		
silk	wvnvgoasdi	soft thread	butrick
silver	talugisdi	shiny, also used for metal. The original word meant reflection.	
sinew	uwadvna		jm351
stockings	diliyo	sock = aliyo	db, jt, jm
striped cloth	tsulaledi		df, db
swan	sgegwa		butrick
tattoo	udoweli	it is marked	jm
tattoos	tsudoweli		
thimble	lesusto		db
thread	asdi		db, df
trunk	ganesaho		db
wampum "Indian beads"	unelsgwaledo		db
weave, he or she is weaving	gvsga		
wool	uwani		

Words given with full syllables. Common pronunciation may shorten them.

Abbreviations in the source column refer to the following authors.
See the Bibliography for full citations.
butrick = Butrick and Brown. db= DeBrahm.
df = Durbin Feeling. dk = Duane King.
jm351 = James Mooney manuscript 351.

Appendix B: English Terms for Cloth and Trims in the 1700s

Names for cloth and trims varied in their use and spelling in the eighteenth century. Here is a brief list (Montgomery 2007, and various sources):

Cloth

Broadcloth was woolen fabric, about fifty-four to sixty-three inches wide, woven in lengths of twenty-four yards. It was woven in the north and west of England and traded around the world.

Calico was cotton fabric named for the city of Calicut in India. Most cotton fabrics of the eighteenth century came from India or France. Calico of the eighteenth century was plain, dyed, or printed with spriggy patterns. It included muslin and chintz. This is not the same as modern calico, a cotton fabric printed with small flowers or patterns close together.

Calimanco was made in England, of wool, and was often brightly colored, with stripes woven into the fabric. Some also had flowers and figures. It was woven in narrow strips about fifteen to eighteen inches wide and thirty yards long.

Cambric was a lightweight fabric, made with a plain weave of fine white linen.

Canvas was woven from hemp and was used to make women's stays, the linings of men's coats, towels, and, in its heaviest form, sails.

Checked fabric was linen with horizontal and vertical stripes woven into it. Some checked fabric was printed. It was made in England, and large quantities were sent to the American colonies. Red, crimson, blue, yellow, and green each had alternating white checks. Some kinds of checked fabric combined colors, making what we would call plaid today.

Chintz originated in India but was being made in England as early as 1726. It was imported to the colonies for clothing and upholstery.

Duffel was woolen cloth made in England, finished in Holland, and mostly shipped to America. Woven a yard and three-quarters wide (63" wide) and thirty yards long, "duffels" were dyed red, blue, or green to satisfy the color preferences of the American Indian tribes. This cloth was heavier than broadcloth or stroud, about the weight of a blanket.

Embossed serge was wool cloth of lighter weight than broadcloth, printed with colorful patterns.

Garlix (or garlick, garlits) refers to linen cloth that was originally made in Görlitz, Silesia, hence its name. It was bleached or unbleached and about seven-eighths of a yard to a yard wide. It was used for shirts and had a wide variety of household applications. It was finer than osnaburg but not as fine as some other linen.

Half thicks were a woolen cloth coarser than broadcloth or Stroud but not as heavy as a blanket.

Holland linen was cloth made from flax in Holland and was white and of fine quality.

India handkerchiefs were silk or cotton, with flowered figures or white figures and dots on a red or indigo background.

Linen refers to any cloth made from flax. Its quality and sources varied widely, but it was the most common fabric at this time. Men's shirts, women's shifts, women's petticoats, short gowns, dresses, handkerchiefs, sheets, tablecloths, napkins, aprons, towels, wallpaper backing, rug backing, needlework backing and more were all made of varieties of linen.

Muslin was lightweight cotton made only in India until the late eighteenth century. It was plain or printed.

Negro cloth was homespun, rather coarse fabric used for the clothing of slaves in the South and in the West Indies.

Osnaburg (or oznabrig) refers to unbleached cloth of linen or hemp, of a coarse weave, originally from the town of Osnabruck, Germany. It was coarser than white linen but not as coarse as a modern burlap bag.

Plaid was a woolen cloth woven with vertical and horizontal intersecting stripes. These were worn by Scottish regiments in the British Army. Traditional patterns of these were locally woven and had been associated with districts or clans in the Highlands of Scotland for many centuries prior to the eighteenth. In 1746 the wearing of any tartan or even the possession of tartan was punishable by death, following the defeat of the Scots by the British at the Battle of Culloden.

Serge was wool cloth of a lighter weight than broadcloth, woven in narrower widths.

Ticking was linen woven with stripes in a twill weave. Common colors were blue and white or tan and white. Ticking was used to line garments but was mainly used to make tents, mattresses, and pillows.

Trims

Caddis (or caddice, cadiz) was a tape or ribbon made of wool for decorative purposes, typically about an inch wide. It was sold and traded in pieces twenty-six yards long. Typical colors were red, dark green, light green, and natural.

Bed lace (or coach lace) refers to tapes for trimming furniture, uniforms, and carriage upholstery. At least an inch wide (and wider), they were woven with figures of the same or contrasting colors. American Indians used this on matchcoats and leggings.

Gold lace is a metal tape woven about half an inch to two inches wide and used on military uniforms and laced hats. It is not like modern lace but is a sturdy tape woven with various patterns in it. Originally, some threads were metal. This was the preferred lace.

Gartering (or gartring) was used by Europeans to tie around the leg just below the knee, much like American Indians did with their traditional garters. This was woven for this purpose, about an inch wide, in plain or patterns, often in combinations of bright colors that included red. Some was patterned like a checkerboard in white with red or white with navy.

None-so-pretty was a general term for tapes or ribbons, of linen or silk, about three-quarters of an inch wide, with woven figures of contrasting colors.

Silk ribbon was part of the deerskin trade and was used by American Indians. It included ribbon from China of various kinds and colors. About an inch or more wide, it was of plain or moire finish, or grosgrain. It was used to tie shirt cuffs, moccasins, and gorgets. It was sewn on match coats, skirts, moccasins, and leggings. Beads were sometimes sewn onto it.

Silver lace was a metal tape woven about half an inch to two inches wide and was used on military uniforms and laced hats. It is not like modern lace but is a sturdy tape woven with various patterns in it. Originally, some threads were metal. This was not as popular as gold lace, because it tarnished.

Appendix C: List of Trade Goods and Prices, 1751

Lists of trade goods and prices provide excellent primary source material from this century, and records are extensive. They come from military sources, Indian agents, colonial governments, and individual traders.

The military gave extensive gifts to Indian allies, including the Cherokees, and had to account for every item. These lists also reflect, at least to some extent, the preferences of the Cherokees and other tribes, who made their preferences known early in the century and traded for or accepted as gifts only the items that they found useful and pleasing. Lists come from the papers of General Amherst, from treaty meetings with the Cherokees and Catawbas, and from the great meeting at Winchester Virginia in 1758, found in the South Carolina papers.

Other useful sources include the papers of John Stuart and Benjamin Hawkins, along with earlier Indian agents. The Colonial Records of South Carolina and the South Carolina Indian Affairs Documents, as well as the records of the Virginia House of Burgesses, yield many accounts of meetings, negotiations, presents, and politics relating to the Indian trade. In numerous repositories, the letters and papers of individual traders of the eighteenth century provide fascinating details. The microfilm collection held at Western Carolina University and the Museum of the Cherokee Indian yields many primary documents of interest in regard to the Indian trade; for more on this subject, see *A Guide to Cherokee Documents in Foreign Archives* (Anderson and Lewis 1983).

Below is the transcription of one of many meetings with a colonial governor, in this case James Glen of the colony of South Carolina. This mid-century document provides a brief glimpse at standard items of the Indian trade and their prices. Taken out of context, however, it would provide a false picture. Troubles with Cherokees and Creeks killing white people in the backcountry occupied much of 1751, with speeches, representatives, and letters passing between the

Cherokee towns and Charlestown. Trade ceased for much of the year, and all parties were anxious to have this matter settled.

This letter and price list, presented on November 1, 1751, was not official until negotiations with the Cherokees were concluded. Later that month Cherokee leaders, both men and women, visited Charleston as an official delegation, received extensive presents (see details in the introduction), engaged in lengthy negotiations and discussions, and finally approved this list, with some changes. Their discussions encompassed law enforcement within and between the Cherokee nation and Great Britain, horse thievery, price gouging by traders who used false weights and measures, boundary lines, problems with settlers in the backcountry, the extent of their powers to negotiate for the people as authorized, and the recently concluded war with the Creeks.

LIST OF THE PRICES OF GOODS FOR THE CHEROKEE TRADE

|173| November 1st, 1751

TO HIS EXCELLENCY, JAMES GLEN, ESQ., AND HONORABLE COUNCIL OF SOUTH CAROLINA, We send this Greeting. We poor, distressed Traders, as your Honorable Council and Assembly has at Present thought proper to bring this Cherokee Trade on a Footing wherewith will endow us to pay our Creditors which know at Present we are Sufferers.

Imprimis. The Prices of Goods if now regulated properly as your Excellency and Council both specified no Stillyards but Scales and Weights to have 1 lb. and 2 lb. Weight, the 1 lb. to be a Deere Skin and 2 lb. to pass a Buck Do., and if a Skin weigh more then 2 Pounds to pass for no more than one Skin.

(McDowell 1758, 146–47).

A Blanket	3 Bucks or 6 Does
2 Yards Strouds	3 Bucks or 6 Does
A Garlix Shirt	2 Do. [ditto] Or 4 Does
Paint, 1 Ounce	1 Doe Skin
Osnbrigs, 1 Yard	1 Do. [ditto]
A Knife	1 Do. [ditto]
A large Knife, buckhandled	1 Buck
1 Pr. Of Hose	1 Buck and one Doe, or 3 Does &c.
Brass Kettles	1 Buck per, or 2 Does
Powder, 3/4	1 Doe
60 Bullets	Ditto
Silver Earbobs	1 Buck the Pair
Pea Buttons, per Dozen	1 Doe
Swan Shott	200 per a Buck Skin
A Steel	1 Doe
A burning Glass	Ditto
Handkerchiefs of India	2 Bucks
Ditto, common	Ditto

1 Riding Sadel [sic]	8 Bucks or 16 Does
2 Yards stript Flannen	2 Bucks or 4 Does
Fine Rufel Shirts [ruffled]	4 Bucks or 8 Does
Women's Side Sadle [sic]	20 Bucks or 40 Does
Men's Shoes	2 Bucks or 4 Does
Callicoes	2 Bucks or 4 Does
Callicoes	Ditto, 1 Buck and 1 Doe, or 3 Does
Fine Ribands	1 Buck 2 Yards, or 4 Does
Gartring	2 Bucks per piece or 4 Does
Caddice Ditto	2 Bucks of 4 Does per piece
2 Yards stompt Flanen	1 Buck and 1 Doe or 3 Does
Worsted Caps	1 Buck and 1 Doe or 3 Does
1 Gun	7 Bucks or 14 Does

Sundry other Goods that may be remitted till a Trader is supplied of what is necessary for his Trade.

Appendix D: List of Trade Goods and Prices, 1762

For	Pounds of skins
Augers, ¾ inch	1½
Augers, 1¼ inch	2½
Bands for Wrist, Silver Plain	
now sent large, Cost 4s:0	7
smaller do. 3s:5	6
Beads, Barley-Corn, now sent large, a Bunch of twelve, short strings	1½
Do. A Bunch of four long Do.	
Bever Trapps, now sent, a large one, with its Chain	15½
a small do. Ditto	11½
Brooches for the Breast, of Silver now sent; which cost 10s a peece	2
Buttons, Breast, of Brass, now sent 36 for	1
Cambrick now sent, which cost about 20s a Yard	3
Duffelds, headed Shagg, now sent, pr. Blanket	5
Frying Pans, a pound	1
Gimblets, small, of all sizes	4
Gloves, men's yarn	1
Gun Locks, now sent, which cost about 15s each	3
Half-thicks, Purple 1¼ yard	2
Hammers, large 1	2
small 1	1
Handsaws 1	4½
Handsaw files 2	½
Handkerchiefs, now sent, Scotch, which cost about 6 or 7p a peece	1
Figured and spotted Do. 9 or 10s Ditto	1½
Silk Ditto 16 or 17s Ditto	3

For	Pounds of skins
Holster Caps, now sent, cost here about £4:5	15
Holsters and Straps, now sent, cost here about £2:15	9
Horse Whips, now sent, cost here about £1:15 a pr.	4
Housings, for Saddles now sent cost here about £2:15 a peece	10
Do. Fringed about £4:10 a peece	15
Juggs, blue and white now sent	
of a Gallon 1	3
of an half-Gallon 1	2
Linnen, now sent, White, about Yard wide which costs about 9 or 10s a yard	1½
Striped Ditto, which costs about 6s/6d a Yard	1
Looking-Glasses Dutch with Cases, now sent	
cost about 11s a peece	3
29s a peece	6
50 s a peece	9
Nails 8d and 10d of either, an hundred	1
2d an hundred	1½
Needles for sewing 50	1
Padlock, small or spring, with Hasp and Staples	1½
Pistols, with brass barrels, now sent, a pair	36
Ribbon, now sent	
Broad Figured Silk which costs about 3s/4d per Yard 2 yards	1
Silk and Cotton Figured costs about 2s/01d per Yard 2½ yards	1
Narrow Taffety, costs about 1s/9d per Yard 3 yards	`
Rope, white 1½ lbs.	1
Saddle now sent, Side for Women; with all Furniture each Saddle	40
Striped Cottons and Cotton-Hollands costs about 11 or 12s a Yard	2
Sleeve, Silver Buttons, costs about 14s a Pair	2½
Shirts, now sent	
white-plain and checked-plain a Peece	7
white-ruffled a Peece	9
checked-ruffled a Peece	8
large (white checked) ruffled for Great Sawny a Peece	9
Stockings, womens Worsted, cost about 16s A Pair	3
Spurs, with Leathers, cost about 9s a Pair	1½
Sugar, Muscovado, now sent Two Pounds	1
Surtout Coats, now sent each	16
Tacks, for Saddles Two hundred	1
Thread, white, now sent an ounce	1
Trunks, Gilt, a Nest containing 7; costs £10; the Whole to be rated proportionally on each Trunk, according to its Size	34

Appendix E: John Vann's License and Inventory, 1765

In 1765 John Vann received a license to trade in the Cherokee Nation. His inventory of goods provides a glimpse into the most common trading items of the time. He listed the total value at 609 pounds, the equivalent of more than $50,000 in 2015 U.S. dollars.

Vann's inventory was made up mostly of cloth and trims, an inventory that seems designed to appeal to Cherokee women. Completely absent are tomahawks, silver armbands, and silver gorgets. These, along with guns, holsters, gun locks, powder, shot, and flints, were prominent in lists of gifts to the Cherokees throughout the 1750s, during the French and Indian War.

A summary of the list confirms Timberlake's observations in 1762 that Cherokees were making their own clothing, except for shirts. Cloth, trim, thread, and buttons dominated Vann's inventory. Wool and linen fabric—plain, printed, checked, and striped—totaled approximately 472 yards. Trims totaled more than 500 yards. Vann also took three dozen men's shirts. He included thread, buttons, handkerchiefs, and blankets.

Note that in the list of goods, a piece of fabric, noted here as "pce" or "pces," is similar in length to a bolt of fabric today, about twenty to thirty yards. Likewise, the pieces of trims—caddis, gartering, none-so-pretty, and ribbons—were twenty to thirty yards. I estimated their length at an average of twenty-five yards each.

Trade items for Cherokee men occupy a small part of this list, unlike in the lists of gifts for Cherokee warriors during the French and Indian War. Vann's inventory includes only 6 guns, along with 200 flints, 1 hundredweight of powder, and 163 weight of bullets. His inventory had a small amount of paint: 10 weight vermilion and 10 weight paint. Eighteen razors were presumably for the men. The three dozen knives in the inventory could have been used by men or women. Two bushels of salt, four large looking glasses, and a gilt trunk rounded out the inventory.

In 1765, only nineteen other traders had licenses or permits to trade throughout the Cherokee Nation. According to the list made by Alexander Cameron, dated Toqueh (Toqua), May 1, 1765, these included: William Little, John Archy, Hugh McGarie, Richard Fields, John Pain, John Walker, John Butler, Dread Peace, John Tally, James Holmes, Alexander Love, John Bowie, Samuel Savage, Samuel Benn, George Downs, Bryan Ward, Samuel Candy, James Walsh, and George Burns. Cameron notes "half breed" after the names John Archy and John Pain (Cameron 1765).

In the 1700s most of the traders married Cherokee women, and these alliances provided benefits to both partners. Traders learned Cherokee language from their wives, used their wives as interpreters, and had the protection of their wives' clans (to a certain extent). Cherokee women participated in the distribution of their husbands' goods and helped set prices. Children of these marriages had the advantages of both parents. Because their mothers were Cherokee, they spoke Cherokee language and belonged to a Cherokee clan; they were considered Cherokee people. Because their fathers were white, they learned English. When grown, some of these children became interpreters, or "linguisters" in the parlance of the eighteenth century. Others became traders, Indian agents, and cultural brokers, occupations that persisted in some of these families well into the nineteenth century.

John Vann's license and inventory are reproduced here. The genealogy of the Vann family in the eighteenth century is the subject of debate. John Vann was either the father or grandfather of James Vann, born 1768, whose mother was Wahli. James became owner of the residence known today as the Vann House. *The Springplace Diaries* (McClinton) identify James Clement Vann, known as "Clem," as young James' stepfather; they identify Wali, Clem's wife, as young James' mother. According to Julia Autry, interpretive ranger at the Vann House State Historic site, Wahli cohabited with both John and James Clement Vann. Young James was the biological son of John but was raised by his uncle James Clement "Clem" Vann. John Vann began trading in the Valley Towns in 1765 and young James was born in 1768. Both John and James Clement Vann participated in some of the actions of Dragging Canoe and his warriors. This may have been the connection that led them to the Chattanooga/northwest Georgia area.

The Vann family amassed a large fortune, and by the early 1800s young James Vann owned more than 1,000 acres of land in present-day northwest Georgia, on which he operated and profited from mills, ferries, toll roads, taverns, and distilleries. Vann also provided land and funding for the first Christian missionaries to the Cherokees, supporting the Moravians so that his and other Cherokee children could learn to read and write English. His house has been restored and is a remarkable historic site.

Note that in the handwriting of these documents, the last name is clearly Vann. In the index to this microfilm, however, the name appears as Nunn, apparently an erroneous reading of eighteenth-century script.

South Carolina

By virtue of a Licence Granted to me by the Honorable Lieut. Governor, in & over Said Province Bearing date June the 4th [illegible] Permitts John Vann to Trade with the Cherokee Indians in the following Econourste Higiwasee Little Tellico, or any other Town in the Valley [illegible] Employ & has given Bond with Sufficient Security as the Law Directs.

This permit [illegible]

Given under my hand & Seal, this 11th Day

Signed –George Parks

True Copy, taken from the Original 11th July 1764

Signed before Edward Wilkinson

& Robinson Sergeant

It appears by the Inclosed amt of Goods sold to John Vann by George Parks that said Vann was to trade by and for himself by virtue of the above permit and that he was not a Substitute or agent for George Parks who [illegible] General License from Lieutenant Governor Bull

J.S. [John Stuart]

- - -

Currett Tail Creek June 25, 1764

Dv [delivered] Jno Vann To George Parks 539.

4 pces Bristol Stroud @ 37 ea.

1 pce Dffl [duffel] Blankets

3 pces Printed Linnen

1 pce Garlix No.4

1 pce Do [ditto] no. 2

1 gross Cadice

½ gross fine Gartering

½ gross Course Do.

3 doz. Men's shirts

1 doz. Large Cutteaus [knives]

2 doz. small Do

2 pces broad Ribbon

2 pces narrow Do

1 pce Oznaburgs

1 small guilt [gilt] trunk

64 yds blue & wt [white] Flannel

10 wt Vermillian

31½ yds red & wt [white] Flannel

1 Oznabridgs Thread

10 wt. Paint

32½ yds. Stripd Holland

35 Ells course Holland

34 Ells Do

2 Bushl Salt

200 Flints

½ Gross Sleeve Buttons

½ doz Rasors

1 gross of none-so-pretty

1 pce Garlix

1 doz blue & wt [white] Handkerchiefs

½ doz. Guns

1 doz. Rasors

163 wt Bullets

100 wt Powder

Duffl blankets

4 Large Looking Glasses

Appendix F: Plants and Animals Used
by the Cherokees for Fiber

common name	Latin name	Cherokee name	part used	how utilized	garments	reference	location
basswood, linden	*Tilia americana*	idehu	inner bark	untreated strips, treated and spun	Iroquois burden strap	Whitford	
canebrake, rivercane	*Arundinaria tecta*	iya	stalk	fiber for rope	moccasins	Whitford	
				splits for baskets			
cattail	*Typha latifolia*				sandals, blanket, mat	Orchard, Whitford	
jute	*Corchorus capsularis*				moccasins	Whitford	
mulberry	*Morus rubra*	kuwv	inner bark	used as strips	skirts	Bartram, Payne	
			inner bark	treated and spun	skirts, mantles, "carpets," nets and fabrics were base for feather capes	DeSoto, Catesby, Adair, et al.	
palmetto	*Sabal palmetto or arecaceae*			cords, baskets		Whitford	
pawpaw	*Asimina triloba*		inner bark?	coarse bags and fabrics		Whitford, Orchard	
richweed	*Pilea pumila*	doleda, dvleda	stalk			Mooney	
yucca	*Eryngium yuccifolium*		leaf	shredded	cords, sandals	Whitford	Kentucky caves

common name	Latin name	Cherokee name	part used	how utilized	garments	reference	location
apocynum family							
Indian hemp, wild hemp	*Apocynum cannabinum*	kadvlati	stem fibers	spun, netted, woven	nets, sandals, fabrics,	Whitford, Orchard, Drooker—skeins in Clifty Creek cave	fabric at Etowah, Georgia east Tennessee
dogbane	*Apocynum androsaemifolium*		stem fibers	spun, netted, woven	nets, fabrics	Whitford	
nettle family							
woods nettle	*Laportea canadensis*		stem	treated, spun, woven	prehistoric skirts in east TN cave	Whitford (1941:13), Drooker (1992:83)	
stingless nettle	*Boehmeria cylindrica*		stem	treated, spun, woven	Cherokee string in feather charm at NMAI, fabric at Etowah	Whitford, Drooker (1992:201)	
slender nettle	*Urtica gracilis*		stem	treated, spun, woven	Iroquois wampum belt	Whitford	
milkweed family							
common milkweed, silkweed, silkgrass	*Asclepias syriaca*	guhi	stem?	spun, woven	threads in Iroquois wampum belt, skirts in NC and VA (PD)	Whitford, Drooker	
					Cherokee fish net	Whitford	
butterfly weed	*Asclepias tuberosa*	unisgahi	stem?	spun, woven	threads in Iroquois wampum belt	Whitford	
non-native species							
cotton	*Gossypium herbaceum*	utsilvi		spun	combined with palmetto in basket, spun and woven after contact	Whitford	
Other plant fiber sources southeastern but not specified Cherokee							
black walnut	*Juglans nigra*	sedi	inner bark fibers	spun into thread		Whitford	
linen	*Linum usitatissinum*			spun		Whitford	
cotton	*Gossypium herbaceum*	utsilvi		spun		Whitford	
slippery elm	*Ulmus fulva*	dawatsila	inner bark	plain fibers, treated and spun	Iroquois burden strap	Whitford	Tennessee caves
slender nettle	*Urtica gracilis*				bag	Whitford	

common name	Latin name	Cherokee name	part used	how utilized	garments	reference	location
Fibers from animal sources—Cherokee							
buffalo hair	*Bison bison*	yansa		spun	garters, belts	Adair, Timberlake	
possum hair	*Didelphis virginiana*	utsesdi	white hair	spun and dyed yellow, red, and black	garters, belts	Payne (v2:138)	
bear hair	*Ursus Americanus*	yona	black hair	spun	black cloth	Payne (v2:128)	
Fibers from animal sources—southeastern but not specified Cherokee							
rabbit	*Sylvilagus floridanus*	tsistu				Drooker	Spiro
dye plants—Cherokee							
bloodroot	*Sanguinaria canadensis*	gili wata					
black walnut	*Juglans nigra*	sedi					
yellow root	*Xanthorhiza simplicissima*	taloni					
butternut, white walnut	*Juglans cinerea*	kohi					
sourwood	*Oxydendron arboretum*	nvdogweya					

Bibliography

"1835 Cherokee Census," Monograph Two. Park Hill: Trail of Tears Association Oklahoma Chapter, 2002.

Adair, James. *The History of the American Indians*. Edited and with an Introduction and Annotations by Kathryn E. Holland Braund. Tuscaloosa: University of Alabama Press, 2005.

Anderson, William L., and James A. Lewis. *A Guide to Cherokee Documents in Foreign Archives*. Native American bibliography series, no. 4. Metuchen, N.J., 1983.

Barbeau, Charles Marius. 1937. *Assomption Sash*. Ottawa: Dept. of Mines, National Museum of Canada. 51 p. (National Museum of Canada bulletin; 75E).

Bartram, William. *William Bartram on the Southeastern Indians*. Edited and annotated by Gregory A. Waselkov and Kathryn E. Holland Braund. Lincoln: University of Nebraska Press, 1995.

———. *Travels*. Athens: University of Georgia Press, 1998.

Baumgarten, Linda. *What Clothes Reveal: The Language of Clothing in Colonial and Federal America*. Williamsburg, Va.: The Colonial Williamsburg Foundation in association with Yale University Press, 2002.

Bender, Margaret. *Signs of Cherokee Culture: Sequoyah's Syllabary in Eastern Cherokee Life*. Chapel Hill: University of North Carolina Press, 2003.

Bradley, Jim. Primary Source of the Month: "Happy While United," Indian Peace Medal by Robert Scot. E-newsletter, Vol. 8, 2009: http://www.history.org.

Butrick, D. S., and D. Brown. *TSVLVKI SQCLVCLV, A Cherokee Spelling Book*. Knoxville, Tenn.: Printed by F. S. Heiskell & H. Brown, 1819.

Cabeza De Vaca, Alvar Nunez. *The Journey of Alvar Nunez Cabeza De Vaca*. Edited by Ad. F. Bandelier. New York: Allerton, 1904.

Catlin, George. *Letters and Notes on the Customs and Manners of the North American Indians in Two Volumes*. New York: Wiley and Putnam, 1842.

Chapman, Jefferson. "Prehistoric American Indians in Tennessee." Frank H. McClung Museum, University of Tennessee, Knoxville Research Notes No. 27, 2009.

———. *Tellico Archaeology*. Knoxville: University of Tennessee Press, 1985.

———, and James Adovasio. "Textile and Basketry Impressions from Icehouse Bottom, Tennessee." *American Antiquity* 42 (1977): 620–25.

Code of Federal Regulations Title 43: Public Lands: Interior. "43 CFR 10.14 Lineal descent and Cultural Affiliation" 2010: http://cfr.vlex.com.

DeBrahm, William Gerard. *De Brahm's Report of the General Survey in the Southern District of North America*. Edited and with an Introduction by Louis De Vorsey Jr. Columbia: University of South Carolina Press, 1971.

Dobyns, H. F. *Their Number Become Thinned*. Knoxville: University of Tennessee Press, 1983.

Drooker, Penelope Ballard. "Mississippian Lace: A Complex Textile Impressed on Pottery from the Stone Site, Tennessee," *Southeastern Archaeology* 10, no. 2 (1991a): 79–97.

———. "Textiles at the Stone Site, Stewart County, Tennessee." Frank H. McClung Museum, The University of Tennessee, Knoxville Research Notes No. 4, March 1991b.

———. *Mississippian Village Textiles at Wickliffe*. Tuscaloosa: University of Alabama Press, 1992.

———, and Laurie Webster, eds. *Beyond Cloth and Cordage: Archaeological Textile Research in the Americas*. Salt Lake City: University of Utah Press, 2000.

Duncan, Barbara R. "The Cherokee War Dance: From Timberlake to the Twenty-First Century." In *Culture, Crisis, & Conflict: Cherokee British Relations 1756–1765*, edited by Anne F. Rogers and Barbara R. Duncan, 83–116. Cherokee: Museum of the Cherokee Indian Press, 2009.

DuPratz, Le Page. *An Account Of Louisiana: Exhibiting a Compendious Sketch of Its Political and Natural History and Topography; With a Copious Appendix Containing Several Important Documents*. New Bern, N.C.: Franklin & Garrow, 1804.

Emery, Irene. *The Primary Structures of Fabrics: An Illustrated Classification*. Washington, D.C.: Textile Museum, 1966.

Etheridge, Robbie, and Sheri M. Shuck-Hall. *Mapping the Mississippian Shatter Zone: The Colonial Indian Slave Trade and Regional Instability in the American South*. Lincoln: University of Nebraska Press, 2009.

Feeling, Durbin, and William Pulte. *Cherokee-English Dictionary*. Tahlequah: Cherokee Nation of Oklahoma, 1975.

Fogelson, Raymond D. "Cherokee in the East." *Handbook of North American Indians*, Vol. 14, *The Southeast*. Washington, D.C.: Smithsonian Institution, 2004.

———. Personal communications, 2010.

Frederickson, N. Jaye. *The Covenant Chain: Indian Ceremonial and Trade Silver*. Ottawa, Canada: National Museum of Man, 1980.

Fundaburk, Emma. *Southeastern Indians Life Portraits: A Catalogue of Pictures, 1564–1860*. Birmingham: Alabama Engraving Company, 1958.

Harding, Deborah. Personal communications, 2005–2011.

Hiroa, Te Rangi (Peter H. Buck). "The Local Evolution of Hawaiian Feather Capes and Cloaks." *Journal of the Polynesian Society* 53, no. 1 (1944): 1–16.

Holmes, William Henry. "Prehistoric Textile Fabrics of the United States, Derived from Impressions on Pottery." *Smithsonian Institution Bureau of Ethnology Annual Report* 3: 393–425. Washington, D.C.: Government Printing Office, 1884.

———. "A Study of the Textile Art In Its Relation to the Development of Form and Ornament." *Smithsonian Institution Bureau of Ethnology Annual Report* 6: 189–252. Washington, D.C.: Government Printing Office, 1888.

———. "Prehistoric Textile Art of the Eastern United States." *Smithsonian Institution Bureau of Ethnology Annual Report for 1891–92* 13: 3–46. Washington, D.C.: Government Printing Office, 1896.

Hudson, Charles. *The Southeastern Indians*. Knoxville: University of Tennessee Press, 1976.

Hutter, Mark. Personal communications, December 2011–January 2012.

Jolie, Edward A., Thomas F. Lynch, Phil R. Geib, and J. M. Adovasio. "Cordage, Textiles, and the Late Pleistocene Peopling of the Andes." *Current Anthropology* 52, no. 2 (2011): 285–296.

Kilpatrick, Jack Frederick. "The Wahnenauhi Manuscript: Historical Sketches of the Cherokees Together With Some of Their Customs, Traditions, and Superstitions."

Anthropological Papers No.77, Bureau of American Ethnology Bulletin 196. Washington, D.C.: U.S. Government Printing Office, 1966.

King, Duane H. *A Grammar and Dictionary of the Cherokee Language.* Athens: University of Georgia, 1975.

Kuttruff, Jenna T., S. Gail DeHart, and Michael J. O'Brien. "7500 Years of Prehistoric Footwear from Arnold Research Cave, Missouri." *Science* 281 (1998): 72–75.

Louis-Philippe, King of France. *Diary of My Travels in America.* New York: Doubleday, 1977.

Mays, Edith. *Amherst Papers, 1756–1763, The Southern Sector: Dispatches from South Carolina, Virginia, and His Majesty's Superintendent of Indian Affairs.* Westminster, Md.: Heritage Books Inc., 2009.

McClinton, Rowena, ed. *Moravian Springplace Mission to the Cherokees.* 2 vols. Lincoln: University of Nebraska Press, 2007.

McDowell, William L. *Documents Relating to Indian Affairs, May 21, 1750–August 7, 1754.* Colonial Records of South Carolina Series 2, Indian books. Columbia, S.C.: 1958.

———. *Documents Relating to Indian Affairs, 1754–1765.* Colonial Records of South Carolina Series 2, v. 3. Columbia, S.C.: 1970.

McKenney, Thomas L., and James Hall. *Indian Tribes of North America.* Philadelphia: E. C. Biddle, 1837.

Mercyhurst College. "South America's oldest textiles identified with carbon dating." ScienceDaily.com. April 13, 2011. Retrieved December 30, 2011: http://www.sciencedaily.com.

Michaux, Andre. *Andre Michaux's Journeys in Oconee County, South Carolina in 1787 and 1788.* Edited by Margaret Mills Seaborn. Walhalla, S.C.: Oconee County Library, 1976.

Montgomery, Florence M. *Textiles in America, 1650–1870.* New York: W. W. Norton, 2007.

Mooney, James. *Myths of the Cherokees: 19th Report of the Bureau of American Ethnology.* Washington, D.C.: U.S. Government Printing Office, 1900.

Museum of the Cherokee Indian. Catesby, Mark, to Hans Sloane, November 27, 1724. Sloan MSS 4047 Fol. 290.

Museum of the Cherokee Indian. James Mooney, "Glossary of Completed Formulae." 564 pages. NAA MS 2536.

Museum of the Cherokee Indian. James Mooney, "Notes on Cherokee Botany." 564 pages. NAA MS 2591.

Museum of the Cherokee Indian. James Mooney, "Upper and Middle Cherokee (Tselaki), vocabulary and kinship charts 1885, 1886 and August–November, 1887." 159 pages. NAA MS 351.

Orchard, William C. *Sandals and Other Fabrics from Kentucky Caves: Indian Notes and Monographs.* New York: Museum of the American Indian, Heye Foundation, 1920.

———. *Beads and Beadwork of the American Indians.* Contributions from the Museum of the American Indian/Heye Foundation, 1975.

Payne, John Howard, and Daniel Sabin Butrick. *The Payne-Butrick Papers, Vols. 1–6.* Edited and Annotated by William L. Anderson, Jane L. Brown, and Anne F. Rogers. Lincoln: University of Nebraska Press, 2010.

Phillips, Joyce B., and Paul Gary Phillips. *The Brainerd Journal; A Mission to the Cherokees, 1817–1823.* Lincoln: University of Nebraska Press, 1998.

Raymond, Margaret. Personal communications, 2006–2007.

Riggs, Brett H. Personal communications, 2015.

Rogers, Anne F., and Barbara R. Duncan, eds. *Culture, Crisis, & Conflict: Cherokee British Relations 1756–1765.* Cherokee: Museum of the Cherokee Indian Press, 2009.

Royce, Charles. *Cherokee Nation of Indians.* Chicago: Aldine Publishing Company, 1975.

Schoeser, Mary. *World Textiles: A Concise History.* London: Thames & Hudson, 2003.

Sibley, Lucy R., Kathryn A. Jakes, and Mary E. Swinker. "Etowah Feather Remains from Burial 57: Identification and Context." *Clothing and Textiles Research Journal* 10 (1992): 21–28.

Standingdeer, John. Personal communication, December 15, 2011.

Stephenson, Robert Scott. *Clash of Empires: The British, French, and Indian War, 1754–1763.* Pittsburgh: Senator John Heinz Regional History Center, 2006.

———. Personal communications, 2005–2011.

Sturtevant, William C. "Louis-Phillipe on Cherokee Architecture and Clothing in 1797." *Journal of Cherokee Studies* 3, no. 4 (1978): 198–205.

Swanton, John Reed. *Indian Tribes of the Lower Mississippi Valley and Adjacent Coast of the Gulf of Mexico.* Washington, D.C.: U.S. Government Printing Office, 1911.

———. *The Indians of the Southeastern United States.* Washington, D.C.: U.S. Government Printing Office, 1946.

Timberlake, Lt. Henry. *The Memoirs of Lt. Henry Timberlake, The Story of a Soldier, Adventurer, and Emissary to the Cherokees, 1756–1765.* Edited by Duane H. King. Cherokee: Museum of the Cherokee Indian Press, 2007.

Ward, Trawick, and R. P. Stephen Davis Jr. *Time Before History: The Archaeology of North Carolina.* Chapel Hill: University of North Carolina Press, 1998.

Whitford, A. C. "Textile Fibers Used in Eastern Aboriginal North America." *Anthropological Papers of the American Museum of Natural History* 38, no. 1 (1941): 1–22.

Williams, Roger. *A Key Into the Language of America.* Reprint, Bedford, Mass.: Applewood Books, 1936.

Witthoft, John. "Dr. John Witthoft Notes Oconaluftee Indian Village 1951." Unpublished manuscript, Museum of the Cherokee Indian Archives, 1951.

———. "Cherokee Beliefs Concerning Death." *Journal of Cherokee Studies* 8, no. 2 (Fall 1983): 68–72.

Wood, Douglas McClure. "'I Have Now Made a Path to Virginia': Outacite Ostenaco and the Cherokee-Virginia Alliance in the French and Indian War." *West Virginia History: A Journal of Regional Studies* 1, no. 1 (2007): 31–60.

Wood, Guy "Darry." "Basic Footwear of the Southeastern Tribes." *Bulletin of Primitive Technology* 19 (2000): 46–56.